SUPPORTING
YOUTH

How to Care, Communicate, and Connect in Meaningful Ways

NANCY TELLETT-ROYCE

Supporting Youth: How to Care, Communicate, and Connect in Meaningful Ways

Nancy Tellett-Royce

The following are registered trademarks of Search Institute: Search Institute®, Developmental Assets®, and

Search Institute Press, Minneapolis, MN
Copyright © 2008 by Search Institute

At the time of publication, all facts and figures cited herein are the most current available; all telephone numbers, addresses, and Web site URLs are accurate and active; all publications, organizations, Web sites, and other resources exist as described in this book; and all efforts have been made to verify them. The author and Search Institute make no warranty or guarantee concerning the information and materials given out by organizations or content found at Web sites that are cited herein, and we are not responsible for any changes that occur after this book's publication. If you find an error or believe that a resource listed herein is not as described, please contact Client Services at Search Institute.

10 9 8 7 6 5 4 3 2 1
Printed on acid-free paper in the United States of America.

Search Institute
615 First Avenue Northeast, Suite 125
Minneapolis, MN 55413
www.search-institute.org
612-376-8955 • 800-888-7828

ISBN-13: 978-1-57482-253-3

Credits
Editor: Alison Dotson
Copy Editor: Mary Byers
Book Design: Percolator
Production Supervisor: Mary Ellen Buscher

Library of Congress Cataloging-in-Publication Data
Tellett-Royce, Nancy.
    Supporting youth : how to care, communicate, and connect in meaningful ways / Nancy Tellett-Royce.
        p. cm.
    Includes bibliographical references and index.
    ISBN 978-1-57482-253-3 (pbk. : alk. paper)
    1. Teenagers and adults. 2. Parent and teenager.
    3. Interpersonal relations in adolescence.
    4. Education—Parent participation. I. Title.
HQ799.2.A35T45 2008
649'.125—dc22
                                      2008021086

About Search Institute Press
Search Institute Press is a division of Search Institute, a nonprofit organization that offers leadership, knowledge, and resources to promote positive youth development. Our mission at Search Institute Press is to provide practical and hope-filled resources to help create a world in which all young people thrive. Our products are embedded in research, and the 40 Developmental Assets—qualities, experiences, and relationships youth need to succeed—are a central focus of our resources. Our logo, the SIP flower, is a symbol of the thriving and healthy growth young people experience when they have an abundance of assets in their lives.

Licensing and Copyright

Contents

Acknowledgments

As I was growing up, I was fortunate to experience many kinds of support from many different adults. I now recognize all the ways my parents supported me, not only when they encouraged me to develop my talents, but also when they pointed out behaviors that were unacceptable, set limits, asked where I was going and when I would be back, or said no when I wanted the answer to be yes.

I grew up in a community that supported the public schools and provided public parks and other safe places for children to play. I remember playing softball across three neighbors' yards and the street out front and knowing that at least one of our mothers was likely to pop her head out to check on us over the course of the evening.

When I became a mother, I realized how relentlessly I had to work at supporting my children. I strived for positive family communication, occasionally saying no when it would have been easier for me to say yes. I made time to support my sons' schools and found safe and challenging extracurricular activities that would help them develop their talents. I engaged with caring adults who all brought their own opinions and worldviews to the conversations they had with my sons.

I am fortunate to have sons who challenged me to adapt and change my parenting strategies as they entered new stages in their own development, and who, along with my husband, Jeff, taught me that family support and communication are interactive processes. I believe I have received much more from them than I have given.

I'd also like to thank my colleagues at Search Institute, who have been willing to engage in many conversations about the roles we play in children's lives, our own and others'. These conversations have shaped my understanding of what the Developmental Assets look like when intentionally applied in real life.

In particular, I would like to thank the publishing staff at Search Institute, especially Susan Wootten, who helped me start this project, and my editor, Alison Dotson, who helped shape this book into something readable. I've learned from both of them that every book is truly a group effort.

Introduction

Kristina was labeled "at risk" by the time she was 8 years old. She lived in poverty, moving from one low-income apartment building to another nearly every year. She grew up in neighborhoods plagued by violence and drug use. By the time she was 11 years old, she was taking care of her four younger siblings as her mother struggled to raise a family on minimum-wage income. Her chaotic childhood took a toll on her schoolwork, resulting in poor grades. If you reduce Kristina to this bleak description of her obstacles, her story sounds hopeless.

So where does a girl like Kristina look for hope?

The first thing Kristina had going for her was her mother, Kathy, who cared deeply about her daughter's future. She publicly praised Kristina's talents and privately talked with her about making better choices than she herself had made. Despite her limited time and resources, Kathy reached out to find free activities and other opportunities for Kristina through the school and local youth programs.

As she and her mother connected with these organizations over the years, Kristina discovered other adults who made it their business to contribute to her success. The program leader of her girls' leadership group coordinated free transportation for all participants. Recreation leaders at her local park gave Kristina's siblings a little extra attention so that she could still spend some time exercising and socializing while she was babysitting. Her school guidance counselor double-checked her mailing address at least once a month to be sure she and her mother were still receiving the information they needed from the school. Later in adolescence, her high school teachers recommended an "alternative" school with flexible hours to accommodate her family's need for Kristina to provide childcare in the mornings. The manager at her fast-food job complimented her strong work ethic and awarded her a promotion at the age of 17.

These individual acts of support did not erase the truly daunting facts of Kristina's adolescence; her relationships with these adults simply gave her a new language for interpreting the events of her life. For example, when three of her four closest friends became pregnant by age 17, she discussed the situation with her mentor and the school guidance counselor, saying, "I've seen how hard my mom works to raise us kids, and I think anyone who has sex in high school is just plain crazy." Unlike the vast majority of her friends and cousins, Kristina avoided pregnancy and sexually transmitted diseases, repeatedly refused drugs, and graduated from high school at the age of 18.

So how does Kristina's story differ from the experiences of many of her peers? Kristina knew and believed that several adults *cared* about her. As people continually stepped in to offer problem-solving guidance or advice, Kristina grew to understand that she had a firm foundation of support holding her up no matter what she faced in life. And here's the best part: No single adult carried sole responsibility, but every adult in her life had the capacity to contribute meaningfully to Kristina's success. Even when there was a "weak link" in this web of support (in this case a lack of involvement from her father), multiple layers of encouragement kept Kristina strong.

This is not a story of impossible expectations. It's not an unrealistic story of a spunky young girl pulling herself up by her bootstraps against all odds. This is a story of *support*. Kristina had support from her mother, her teachers, her neighborhood park workers, her youth program leaders, her boss—all of the significant adults in her life. In big and small ways, these individuals provided the love and encouragement she needed to grow into a healthy adult.

NO YOUNG PERSON DESERVES to feel invisible, unrecognized, or unnamed. All young people need caring, supportive adults in their lives. Sometimes it appears that young people are seeking just the *opposite* of adult support and want to tackle life with only their peer group by their side, but even if young people don't come right out and ask for support, they are looking for adults around them who can provide it.

How can you support the young people in your life?

Search Institute's Developmental Assets framework identifies 40 strength-based qualities, skills, and values that adults can provide for or nurture in young people to help them thrive. The first six assets define the category "Support" and address the various contexts—family, neighborhood, school, and broader community of caring adults—across which young people need to experience support in order to succeed in becoming healthy, caring, and responsible. Both common wisdom and research help us understand how important these assets are in a young person's life, and offer insight into how we can best build these assets for and with the young people with whom we work and come into contact.

RESEARCH ON SUPPORT

Search Institute research scientists observe that the three Support assets linked to parents (Asset 1: Family Support, Asset 2: Positive Family Communication, and Asset 6: Parental Involvement in Schooling) have been associated with positive outcomes such as lower rates of substance abuse, delinquency, and early sexual intercourse, and higher levels of academic performance

Patricia Hersch, author of *A Tribe Apart,* spent three school years following eight teens and their friends through the ups and downs of their daily lives. Because teens create their own culture, Hersch describes them as "a tribe apart," but she sees this separation as a result of adults pulling away from young people, not the other way around. She maintains that teens aren't receiving the supervision or the recognition they need from adults. In her epilogue, Hersch writes about a visit she had from Jonathan, one of the eight students:

> *He came in, followed me into my office, folded his lanky body into the cozy easy chair while I went and got our customary glasses of ice water. We went on, as usual, for hours. Before he left, he lifted himself up to get out of the chair, then sat down again. His face was set in that thoughtful look I had often seen just before he said something of special importance.*
>
> *"Talking to you has helped me tremendously," he said. "Nobody has a chance to really talk to anybody about what they are thinking."* [1]

After years of building a relationship with Patricia, Jonathan was able to articulate the deep need teens have for adults to accept and listen to them. Many teens may not be able to recognize this need, but they will look for clues that the adults around them are caring and supportive.

If you are parenting a teenager, how can you balance his need to make decisions more independently with your desire to ensure his safety? How can you grow into this new role of parenting a teen, which calls for engaging in uncomfortable conversations, trying to model the behavior you expect of him, and learning not to take occasional outbursts personally? Understanding how the Support assets can be built in a young person's life can serve as a foundation.

If you are a teacher or program provider, how do you make your support clearly available? Do you . . .

- make yourself available for one-on-one conversations with young people in your school or after-school program?

- pause during a prepared activity or lesson to make time for conversation if the group seems upset or excited by some external event?

- ask questions and get to know the individual teens in your program?

- look for opportunities to help them build the interpersonal skills that will enable them to make friends of both peers and adults?

- recognize and acknowledge their talents, the gifts that make them uniquely themselves? Young people notice when adults reach out to them.

As an adult seeking to provide meaningful support to young people, you can begin by looking back. Ask yourself which caring adults showed up in your young life. What did they do to make you feel special? How did they support you? Taking time for this kind of reflection can help you ground your understanding of support in your own experiences growing up.

Consider the following scenario: A youth-serving professional is leading a session with community members, defining the Developmental Assets as a web of support every young person needs. She asks the group of adults to reflect on who was there for them when they were growing up.

The room immediately begins to buzz as each audience member shares memories with the person next to them. An older woman remembers a high school teacher who encouraged her to write. A man remembers a time when he and his father argued over something, the topic long forgotten, and his father said, "I will always love you, no matter what." The memory is still powerful enough to cause a catch in the man's voice as he recounts the story.

Another young man talks about how frequently his parents fought when he was younger, and how he found an escape by visiting his next-door neighbor, who was always working on his car in the garage. Over the years, the neighbor explained how carburetors worked and what gear ratios were, but what the young man remembered most was how safe he felt in that garage . . . how the outside world vanished . . . how any question he asked was considered and answered, and how he felt accepted, valued, and respected.

The group leader calls for more examples, and adults mention grandparents, coaches, Sunday school teachers, and bus drivers who always smiled and greeted them by name.

Every adult has the power to exert a strong influence in the life of a teen. This power is not dependent on financial status. It does not rely on an advanced degree in child psychology or social work or education. It is not dependent on age, gender, race, or religion. All that matters is that you seize each opportunity to be intentionally present in the lives of young people.

We were all young once.

As we move through adulthood, our memories of events in our own childhood change. Although we may think we remember what it was like to be a teenager, chances are good that our recollections have faded or we have reinterpreted them through our adult eyes. For young people around us, their experiences are vivid, immediate, and not yet tempered by 20/20 hindsight. For these reasons as well as others we need to really *listen* to young people to understand what's affecting their lives.

What This Book Can Do for You

Whether you work with youth on a daily basis or your interaction with young people is less formal and less frequent, there have most likely been times when you haven't known exactly what to say or how to act, so you've said and done nothing. You *want* to reach out to teens—you want to listen, offer support and encouragement, and be a positive influence—but it's not always easy. This book will help you communicate more deeply and effectively with the young people in your life, whether they be your own children, your neighbors, customers at your workplace, students, or players on the team you coach.

Each chapter has three sections: "In My Family," "In My Professional Life," and "In My Community." Each section offers concrete advice and actions you can take to support youth in every area of your life. If you are a parent, you might find yourself most interested in the family sections; if you are a youth leader, you may benefit more from the professional sections; and whatever your role, you can apply tips from the community sections. You might even find you're able to apply tips from all three sections. At the end of each chapter, you'll find two asset-building activities you can use with groups of youth. You can build assets for youth everywhere from your own home to your community at large. Make this book work for you and the youth in your life!

Search Institute's Framework of 40 Developmental Assets® for Adolescents (ages 12 to 18)

Search Institute® has identified the following building blocks of healthy development—known as Developmental Assets—that help young people grow up healthy, caring, and responsible.

EXTERNAL ASSETS

Support

1. **Family Support**—Family life provides high levels of love and support.

2. **Positive Family Communication**—Young person and her or his parent(s) communicate positively, and young person is willing to seek advice and counsel from parent(s).

3. **Other Adult Relationships**—Young person receives support from three or more nonparent adults.

4. **Caring Neighborhood**—Young person experiences caring neighbors.

5. **Caring School Climate**—School provides a caring, encouraging environment.

6. **Parent Involvement in Schooling**—Parent(s) are actively involved in helping young person succeed in school.

Empowerment

7. **Community Values Youth**—Young person perceives that adults in the community value youth.

8. **Youth as Resources**—Young people are given useful roles in the community.

9. **Service to Others**—Young person serves in the community one hour or more per week.

10. **Safety**—Young person feels safe at home, at school, and in the neighborhood.

Boundaries & Expectations

11. **Family Boundaries**—Family has clear rules and consequences and monitors the young person's whereabouts.

12. **School Boundaries**—School provides clear rules and consequences.

13. **Neighborhood Boundaries**—Neighbors take responsibility for monitoring young people's behavior.

14. **Adult Role Models**—Parent(s) and other adults model positive, responsible behavior.

15. **Positive Peer Influence**—Young person's best friends model responsible behavior.

16. **High Expectations**—Both parent(s) and teachers encourage the young person to do well.

Constructive Use of Time

17. **Creative Activities**—Young person spends three or more hours per week in lessons or practice in music, theater, or other arts.

18. **Youth Programs**—Young person spends three or more hours per week in sports, clubs, or organizations at school and/or in the community.

19. **Religious Community**—Young person spends one or more hours per week in activities in a religious institution.

20. **Time at Home**—Young person is out with friends "with nothing special to do" two or fewer nights per week.

INTERNAL ASSETS

Commitment to Learning

21. **Achievement Motivation**—Young person is motivated to do well in school.

22. **School Engagement**—Young person is actively engaged in learning.

23. **Homework**—Young person reports doing at least one hour of homework every school day.

24. **Bonding to School**—Young person cares about her or his school.

25. **Reading for Pleasure**—Young person reads for pleasure three or more hours per week.

Positive Values

26. **Caring**—Young person places high value on helping other people.

27. **Equality and Social Justice**—Young person places high value on promoting equality and reducing hunger and poverty.

28. **Integrity**—Young person acts on convictions and stands up for her or his beliefs.

29. **Honesty**—Young person "tells the truth even when it is not easy."

30. **Responsibility**—Young person accepts and takes personal responsibility.

31. **Restraint**—Young person believes it is important not to be sexually active or to use alcohol or other drugs.

Social Competencies

32. **Planning and Decision Making**—Young person knows how to plan ahead and make choices.

33. **Interpersonal Competence**—Young person has empathy, sensitivity, and friendship skills.

34. **Cultural Competence**—Young person has knowledge of and comfort with people of different cultural/racial/ethnic backgrounds.

35. **Resistance Skills**—Young person can resist negative peer pressure and dangerous situations.

36. **Peaceful Conflict Resolution**—Young person seeks to resolve conflict nonviolently.

Positive Identity

37. **Personal Power**—Young person feels he or she has control over "things that happen to me."

38. **Self-Esteem**—Young person reports having a high self-esteem.

39. **Sense of Purpose**—Young person reports that "my life has a purpose."

40. **Positive View of Personal Future**—Young person is optimistic about her or his personal future.

1

FAMILY SUPPORT

Family life provides high levels of love and support.

Sixty-eight percent of young people in grades 6 through 12 report experiencing this asset in their lives.

This information is based on data collected on 148,189 students surveyed in 2003 using *Search Institute Profiles of Student Life: Attitudes and Behaviors*.

Families come in all sizes and configurations. They may include one parent or two parents, stepparents, grandparents, aunts, uncles, biological parents, foster parents, adoptive parents, or any other adults parenting by choice. Families can include one child or multiple children who may or may not be related biologically. Throughout this book, the term "parent" will be used to represent any adult who steps into the critical role of parenting children.

Whatever their makeup, families are the context in which children first learn whether the world is safe and predictable or scary and unsure. Parents are at the center of a young child's universe, and even as young people grow into their teen years, they continue to need to know they are loved and supported by these central figures in their lives.

When love and support are present, children grow into adolescents who can trust others and build solid friendships, and as they move forward into adulthood, they have the ability to build sustained intimate relationships and form their own family units. When those early bonding experiences are missing, a young person may have trouble trusting others and may shy away from sustained relationships when he reaches adulthood. Interestingly, researchers have noted that closeness in the family does not prevent a young person from becoming independent, but actually prepares him for independence by providing him with emotional strength.

Researchers characterize family or parental support along dimensions of warmth, firmness, and democracy.[2] This means parents are emotionally close to and communicate openly with their children, provide clear but occasionally negotiable boundaries, and engage in discussions of family rules. In a study of some 10,000 high school students, only 20 percent of the young people said they experienced this kind of parental support.[3]

In My Family

Much of what we bring to our understanding of family support comes from our own experience of being a child in a family. Think back on your earliest memories of your family and the many interactions you had with your parents and other family members over the years. Now reflect on the following questions:

- How do I know my family loved me?
  - What did they say?
  - What did they do?

- Could I count on my family for help and support if I needed it?

- What is one example of a time I needed help and received it?

- Did I get along well with my parent(s) or the adults who raised me?

- Did we discuss things openly in my family, or did my parent(s) set all the rules?

- Are there times I remember just hanging out and being with my family, or are all my memories about *doing* things?

You may be smiling as you remember the times you felt most supported by your family. Or you may be feeling sadness or anger over what you feel was missing in your family as you grew up. We all respond at a deep emotional level when we think about our earliest memories of "family." Whatever your experience, you can now work to build support in your own family.

Getting Started

Parenting can be exhausting, and it's easy to lose focus. Refer to this grid periodically to evaluate your parenting and remind yourself to be the best parent possible. The great news is that every day is an opportunity to start anew.

This Week I . . .	Mon	Tues	Wed	Thurs	Fri	Sat	Sun
Told my child that I love her.							
Took time to look my child in the eye and named something positive I saw in him.							
Made time for just the two of us.							
Ate a meal with my child.							
Asked my child how she would like to be supported, and I followed through.							

Use the information from the grid to set a goal for today or for the week. Which of the strategies did you find most difficult? What would help you remember to act on that strategy?

If you find yourself struggling to act on your chosen strategy consistently, use one or more of the following reinforcements:

- If there is another adult in your household, tell her about the goal you have set for yourself and ask her to check in with you daily to help you stay on track.

- Select one strategy from the grid. Start a conversation at the dinner table. Let all family members know you are committed to being more consistent in working toward that goal. Tell them that every one of them has the power to build the asset of family support, and ask if they would like to tackle any strategies from the grid or one of their own choosing. Periodically check in with each other to see how it is going.

Research on behavior change suggests that it takes 28 days of repetition to solidify a new behavior and make it a habit. Remember this whenever you feel frustrated and consider giving up.

Now think about your children. Have you noticed changes in them that would suggest they are moving into a new phase of development? For example: They are now doing chores without being reminded; completing homework on their own, or mastering a subject they used to struggle with; asking you about staying up later or out later; dating or using the car; or challenging family rules they used to follow without question.

It is important to notice these changes in our children. Sometimes our response as a parent is frustration. The rules we set don't fit so well anymore. The parenting strategies we were getting comfortable with seem to be losing their effectiveness. Our first impulse may be to try to ignore or stifle our children's changing behavior. This won't work, because it's their "job" as children to go through a series of developmental changes. As parents we can choose to celebrate these signs of healthy growth and development even as we begin to search for different strategies and structures we can use to support this new phase of our child's development.

Some parents fear what lies ahead and hang back, hoping they can stick with the old ways of doing things. Others assume that a new stage means they no longer have responsibility to monitor and negotiate behaviors. Somewhere in the middle lies the path of the supportive parent. Supportive parents watch for signs of change and negotiate and adjust to find new ways to be in a healthy relationship with their children.

Time to Bond

Sometimes parents can get so wrapped up in the stress of day-to-day life that it becomes challenging to slow down and just enjoy their children. Whether you have young children or teenagers, you can look for creative ways to connect. The goal is not to complete any specific activity but to create opportunities for shared experiences and conversations. Try any of the following ideas to bond with your child:

Lie on a blanket on the grass and look for shapes in the clouds.

Play one-on-one basketball.

Take your child out for a Saturday morning pancake breakfast, or buy the ingredients on Friday night and make pancakes at home. Have your child pick out toppings or fillers for the pancakes—strawberries, blueberries, chocolate chips—and make your pancakes in different shapes with cookie cutters depending on your mood or the season.

Choose flowers or vegetables to plant in a garden together. Work on weeding and talk about what you can do with your harvest, whether you are growing flowers or vegetables.

Teach your child an old card game you have always enjoyed, and have your child teach you a card game you may have never played.

Play video games with your child, and take turns picking the game. Where appropriate, discuss the pros and cons of various games.

Listen to music. Take turns choosing the music. Ask only positive questions: What does this song mean to you? How does this music make you feel? What is your favorite song?

Start a conversation about rules in the family. Share rules you live by. Ask your child's opinion of the rules she has to follow. Listen to her opinion.

Work on a jigsaw puzzle or play a strategy game together. If you have room to spread out in your home, get a 1,000-piece jigsaw puzzle. You can work on it once a night or even once a week. A scheduled 15-minute session can easily turn into a few hours spent chatting or working in companionable silence together.

Have a home spa day. Experiment with different hairstyles and nail polishes.

Organize family photos. Keep it simple by using a photo album with sleeves, or really get into it by making a colorful scrapbook or poster. Take turns telling the stories that go with the pictures. Children's memories are shaped by the way in which we retell our family stories. Look for ways to name a strength, find signs of growth, or remember fun times.

One teen remembers a day when she and her mother were looking through family pictures and they came across one of herself at 3 years old, wearing three pairs of pants and four T-shirts. She says her mother reacted by saying, "Even when you were young you had a flair for individuality," instead of a more negative statement such as, "You could never make up your mind about what to wear."

Another family remembers how a photo of the father and his two sons throwing snowballs at each other created a fun bonding moment and triggered more memories. The younger son said, "Remember how we made a snow fort together that year the snow was so deep?"

Parenting from a Distance

For many reasons, sometimes parents must spend extended periods away from their children. Children need as many caring adults as possible in their lives. Families in which the parents live apart because of divorce or separation should try to keep their child's best interests at heart as they weigh various choices about custody and visitation. Parenting is not a competitive sport, so don't make your child choose sides. Unless there are safety concerns, it is most beneficial for children to stay connected to both parents.

Sometimes parents deal with their own pain over a separation by avoiding communication. Children want a connection, even if they are physically apart from their parents. Try to be as predictable as possible and call your children at a regular time each day or week. You can also keep in touch by writing a weekly note, e-mail, or letter; sharing a funny story from your week; or reading the same book or watching the same TV show as your children and discussing it in your phone calls, e-mails, or letters. For other suggestions on how to stay in touch, see Tenessa Gemelke, *Stay Close: 40 Ways to Connect with Kids When You're Apart* (Search Institute, 2005).

Make a care package that you can either deliver in person or by mail depending on where your children live. Personalize the care package by applying themes based on holidays, the season, or your child's interests:

Does your child love to read? Send a small package with a book, book light, bookmark, and a small homemade blanket.

How about games and activities? Create a care package that includes a pack of cards; a book of crossword puzzles, word jumbles, or drawing activities; and some colorful pens, pencils, or markers.

If your child loves sports, send a pocket biography of her favorite athlete, cards or other collectibles, a bottle of Gatorade, and, depending on her favorite sport, a baseball, jersey, or homemade "team" shirt. Make a coupon that your child can redeem on your next visit with each other. You can promise to take her to a game or, even better, to play catch, run laps at the school track, or go for a swim together.

Treat your child to a movie night. Include a video or DVD, a package of microwave popcorn, napkins with his favorite movie characters on them, or a small poster or card of his favorite actor or movie.

Include small reminders from a family vacation or trinkets from a shared hobby.

At Halloween, include candy, a small pumpkin or gourd, fake spiders, a scary or funny mask and accessories, and lollipop ghosts (you can make your own with toilet paper, tape, and a black marker for spooky eyes).

Don't worry that you'll have to spend a lot of money—your child will appreciate the homemade touches you have added and likely won't care if you bought items from a dollar store or garage sale. The goal is to regularly remind your child that you are thinking about her or him.

The Language of Love

All parents want their children to be happy, and it is easy to confuse what your children *want* with what they *need*. Television commercials and magazine ads encourage children to ask for toys, clothes, and other items that will supposedly make them popular and happy, and parents often feel pressured to buy things that can help their children fit in. The good news is that you can help your children feel loved and supported without depending on money or material things.

It is never too late to start expressing your love to your children, and any way you choose to do so is a step in the right direction. You can show your children your love with words and actions. Try any of the following ways to tell your children you love them:

SAY IT

Agree to use a code word or phrase if your kids get embarrassed when you say "I love you" in public. Even a quote from a movie becomes special when you define a secret meaning for it.

Tell your kids you love them as they head off to school in the morning. Say "I love you" when you tuck them in at night or before they go to their bedrooms for the evening.

Use terms of endearment when you talk to your children. Adding a childhood nickname or sweet term to your good-byes, hellos, and requests will remind your kids that no matter how old they get, they are still special to you.

Share stories from your kids' early months or years of your life together. They will sense how much you love them when they see how much you enjoy talking about all of their firsts, the funny things they said or did, and how happy you were when they were born or when you adopted them.

Even if they respond with, "Yeah, I know" or "You don't need to tell me," say it anyway! Secretly, they will be pleased.

WRITE IT

If your teen has a cell phone, send a supportive text message when you know she'll be on the school bus, over her lunch hour, or before a big game or concert.

Some young people are more receptive to written communication. Send thoughtful e-mails and sign them with "Love, Dad [or Mom, or your name]."

Write "I love you" on a slip of paper and tuck it in with his lunch, or write it on the inside edge of his lunch bag. Slip a note under his bedroom door or write it in the shower mist on the bathroom mirror, where it becomes a secret message.

Leave a note on her pillow, by her toothbrush, anywhere you know she'll see it.

MAKE IT YOUR OWN

Learn how to say "I love you" in sign language so you can flash it to your children in public without embarrassing them.

Use humor to bond with your children—they will love sharing inside jokes with you.

Practice empathy. If your daughter comes to you because she had food stuck in her braces all day and no one told her, or your son tripped on the stairs in front of someone he has a crush on, first listen, and then lighten the situation by sharing an embarrassing moment of your own.

SHOW IT

Tuck a blanket around your child if he falls asleep on the couch on a Sunday afternoon.

Hug your children often, even when they say they're too old for your affection.

Make her favorite breakfast on days when you know she has a big test or event coming up. Even if her favorite breakfast is cereal, make sure you have her favorite kind on hand.

DISCUSS IT

Every child and every family is different, and children can feel differently about various expressions of love at different stages of their lives. When you have a moment for a quiet conversation, ask your children how they know that you love them. If you have caught them at a moment when they aren't feeling particularly loved or lovable, don't stop there. Tell them you *do* love them and you want their help in finding ways to let them know it.

Ask for their suggestions. One teen told his father that public hugs were out, but that a gentle punch on the shoulder would be all right when they were outside the home.

Share with them how you know they love you and value you, too. Some children can verbalize their feelings more easily than others. Acknowledge that there are nonverbal ways that you notice them demonstrating their love, too. ("Thanks for making me that picture . . . Thanks for watching your little brother when I had to go to work . . . Thanks for putting gas in the car after you borrowed it.")

Encourage them to show love to their siblings as well. Every member of the family can play a role in building family support. When an older sibling, cousin, or other family member makes a special effort to spend time with a young person, it benefits them both. The young person will feel supported, and the older youth will feel useful and proud to be a caring older person in a younger child's life.

No matter how your own family of origin interacted, as a parent you can make the choice to **model and ask for respectful, caring behavior between family members,** and you can reinforce these positive behaviors.

Family relationships will grow deeper when you take the time for these conversations, even if they feel a little awkward at first. Your children will appreciate your efforts when they see you working to be a more intentional part of their lives.

Brothers and Sisters

"Dad likes me best!"

In any family with more than one child, it is common for each child to look for signs that she or he is valued most. Telling your children that you love them all the same isn't necessarily your best strategy, but it *can* help to remind them that there is enough love in the family for everyone. Think about each of your children's unique qualities and strengths, and make sure you affirm them. At the same time, you can teach your kids that "fairness" doesn't necessarily mean that each child gets exactly the same amount of attention or the same treatment. For example, a 6-year-old and a 14-year-old both need some undivided attention from their parents or the adults who are raising them, and a child with special needs may need many more hours of attention than a child without those special needs, but all children need to know they are seen, valued, loved, and affirmed in their family. This may mean that you find respite care so you can book some one-on-one time with the child without special needs, or that you set aside some time after the 6-year-old is in bed to give undivided attention to the 14-year-old.

If you aren't sure whether this is an issue in your family, have separate conversations with each child. For example, you can remind your older daughter that even though you've been focusing a lot of attention on her younger brother you haven't forgotten her and still love her. Ask her how she feels and if she has any ideas for an activity the two of you could do together.

In My Professional Life

Whether you're a teacher, youth program leader, or another adult who cares about kids' well-being, you can have an impact on their family support systems—even if they're not a part of your own family.

If You're a Teacher

Think about ways you can occasionally turn homework into an opportunity for family time. Elementary schools have created "Math Cases" or "Math Bags." Each is packed with a mix of playing cards, a cribbage board, dominoes, math puzzles, and instruction cards to help families play together. Circulate the games among class members throughout the year.

If you work with older students, look through the middle school and senior high curricula for opportunities to create shared family experiences, such as discussing current events or critiquing TV commercials. Almost every topic has the potential to help young people connect more deeply with their families.

Whoever You Are!

Engage young people with the following activities and exercises, whether they're the students in your classroom or the youth in your after-school program. These activities invite young people to reflect on their families, and they are flexible enough to include kids who are adopted or are in foster care. Use care when administering the family crest or family history interview activities. Whenever possible, keep the discussions current and have teens reflect on their most immediate family members.

Encourage young people to design a family crest with four illustrations that represent things that are important to them about their families. Have them share their crest with their family.

Have young people conduct a family history interview. Create questions that get families sharing stories with each other. Depending on the age of the young person, they can ask family members about the origins of their favorite sayings as well as *all* their favorites: food, activities, sports, and music. Youth can also create a family tree. For ideas, visit www.familytree.com or www.familysearch.org.

Have group members name ways each member of their family shows them support, and encourage them to let family members know how much they appreciate those actions. Discuss possible gestures they could initiate, such as writing a thoughtful letter, recording a mix of special songs, or cleaning the living room.

Ask them to identify one or two ways they wish some member of their family showed support, and prompt them to think about how they might ask for it. Remind them that this is not about material things or money, but other kinds of support such as wise words and caring actions.

Have them identify three ways they show support to each of their family members. Suggest they think of one new way they could surprise a family member by showing support.

If you invite guest speakers to your youth program, ask them to share how their families supported them in reaching their goals or becoming the person they are now.

> For great tips to share with a teen on how to work on family support and communication, see Peter L. Benson, Judy Galbraith, and Pamela Espeland, *What Teens Need to Succeed: Proven Practical Ways to Shape Your Own Future* (Free Spirit Publishing, 1998).

Overcoming Barriers to Family Support

You may work with youth who seem to receive no support from their family. Maybe you know an extremely bright teenager whose parents don't appear to value education, or maybe you've met a young gay man who is afraid to discuss his sexual orientation with his parents. Help young people explore their options for family support. Why do they have trouble connecting with their parents? Can they reach out to a grandparent, a sibling, or an aunt or uncle who can offer the support they need? Let young people know that there are many adults outside their family who can help them fill this gap, and that you will help them connect with other caring adults. If the youth *does* ask for your help in finding these supportive adults, make sure you follow through—doing what you say is a very important lesson to model for young people and one that, in our fast-paced world, is easy to let slip by.

In order to have this type of conversation it helps to know a young person fairly well. This is why spending time getting to know young people as individuals is so critical to their development. When we can name and affirm the uniqueness of a young person, they may be more open to our efforts to offer assistance. Remember, too, that sometimes our offer to help can make a big difference, even if the young person can't verbalize it or seems to shrug it off. This challenge is covered in more depth in Chapter 3, Other Adult Relationships.

How Can You Encourage Parents to Build This Asset?

If you work directly with parents, or communicate with the parents of young people who are in your classroom or program, you have many opportunities to let them know how important family support is to a young person. In a survey carried out by Search Institute and the YMCA of the USA, researchers found that 53 percent of parents felt they were "going it alone" and could identify no one they turned to for support, but 80 percent strongly agreed there was always something more they could learn about being a good parent. When asked what would help them as parents, the number one answer was having people tell them they're doing a good job. This is one simple way you can build family support whether you have children or not. (To read *Building Strong Families,* the survey report, go to www.search-institute. org/families.)

If you work with children, communicate with their parents and encourage them to extend the learning or activity you presented during the day. For example, offer activities they can do at home and share some conversation starters they can use to get their child talking about the activity. Remember, though, how important it is for families to have unstructured time together. Don't overschedule the evening time of children in your program or classroom.

Encourage parents to take time for themselves. If parents are well rested, energized, and satisfied in their own lives, they will be much better equipped to give their children the support they need. If you send out a newsletter or flyers, include ideas for parent-friendly activities now and then. Simply reminding parents that it's beneficial for them to see a movie, go out to dinner, or take walks without their kids will go a long way toward building a healthy and well-balanced home environment.

Expanding the Web of Support

Many parents have times when they feel they are going it alone. You can help parents feel more connected to other parents and build family support.

Encourage parents to arrive a little early now and then when they pick up their children so they can have conversations with other parents. Make it easier for them by picking a night when you can provide coffee and snacks or treats.

If you have children of your own, **talk to the parents sitting next to you** at your child's sports practices and events.

Host a potluck supper at the beginning or end of your program series, or organize a block party. Contact your city to find out what support it offers for block parties and what regulations apply.

Check with your school district's Community Education program, the local YMCA or YWCA, library, or your congregation for programs they offer for parents and **post the information where parents can see it.**

Coordinate parent education events for the parents of your students or the youth in your program.

If you gather parents as a group (for open houses, sign-up events, classes), allow for "mingling time" so they can get to know each other better. The more comfortable parents are in these settings, the more likely they'll be to support each other outside the program or school setting. Print and distribute a parent and child phone list, which makes it possible for parents to connect with each other outside their child's class or group setting.

Sponsor an event where families can do something fun together and get to know the other families in your program. If you can't do this yourself, assemble a list of family-friendly places in the community where parents and their children can volunteer together or participate in activities as a family. Your local United Way or Volunteer Center can assist you in identifying these opportunities in the community.

If you like to organize events, contact your city to **get information on block parties.** Find out what support the city offers and what the regulations are for block parties.

Building a Family-Friendly Work Environment

If you employ parents in your workplace, discuss whether or not you have family-friendly practices and ask employees for suggestions that would make your workplace more supportive of families. Even organizations that work with young people and families sometimes fail to look at their own employment practices through a family-friendly lens.

Every year, *Working Mother* magazine names the top 100 companies for working mothers. Companies that believe they qualify for the list submit an extensive application. Seven categories are measured: workforce profile, compensation, child care, flexibility, time off and leaves, family-friendly programs, and company culture.

Wondering what benefits these companies offer? The Allstate Corporation features an on-site child-care center as well as five near-site centers; General Mills allows its employees to take up to six months of unpaid personal leave; and Merck boasts a softball field, basketball court, jogging trails, and tennis courts. (To read more about the other 97 companies, visit workingmother.com.)

Sound ambitious? Even if your company has limited resources, you can implement small changes that will make significant differences in the family lives of your employees.

- Allow for more flexible schedules for all employees, including nonparents. Doing so will not only allow parents to attend school events and doctor appointments, it will also boost morale for everyone in the company.

- Provide a private space for nursing mothers to express milk.

- Organize an annual family picnic.

- Keep toys and games on hand for children who visit the office.

- When older children visit the office, occupy them with tasks they might like to help out with, such as stuffing and applying labels to envelopes.

- If you offer employee education programs over the lunch hour, bring in an occasional speaker who can address parenting issues. Your local early childhood organizations or Community Education office can help you locate an expert.

These practices will help create a warm and caring atmosphere that even those without children will appreciate. The good news for your organization is that it may benefit from better employee attendance and loyalty.

Support Your Coworkers Who Are Parents

- Acknowledge that parenting is hard work. Note any strengths or progress you see in their parenting.

- Ask parents what kinds of information or support would be most helpful, and work with them to find it.

- Talk to parents about what they enjoy most about their family.

- Encourage them to take care of themselves. (For tips, distribute the pocket-sized poster "Raising Kids with Care: 50 Ways to Help Your Whole Family Thrive" from Search Institute.)

Elizabeth Vargas of ABC made the difficult decision to give up her anchoring job with *World News Tonight* in favor of a more forgiving work schedule with *20/20* after the birth of her second child. Her first assignment for *20/20* was a special report on working moms in the United States. She was surprised to learn how resentful some nonparents are of their coworkers who are parents.

She told Oprah, "Listen, I have to tell you. I was in the workforce as a childless woman for 20 years. I had no clue how hard it was for my colleagues who were parents all that time until I became one. I just have to say it's really hard to imagine until you're actually in that position." [4]

In My Community

Children and teens are all around you. They live in your neighbor-hood. They bag your groceries. They attend your church, synagogue, or mosque. They sit in the backseat while you carpool them to soccer and swimming lessons. They shop at many of the same stores you do. It may be hard to see how you can help build this asset of Family Support for children who don't live under your roof, but there are many ways you can contribute.

Is Your Community Family-Friendly?

Ask yourself the following questions about your community:

Are there parks, recreation centers, walking or biking paths, and other public spaces where families can spend time together outside their home and in the community? If the answer is no, talk to local officials about the need for public spaces that are family-friendly.

Are there safe routes young people can use to get to the ballpark, their school, or neighborhood parks? If they have to travel on heavily trafficked roads or along unlit paths, bring this to the attention of local planners or officials. Parents often have to change work plans or juggle their schedules to ensure that their children can get to extracurricular activities safely. Community members can play a role in attending to these safety issues for the youngest members of their community and, by doing so, make their communities more family-friendly.

Do nonparents in your community support their local schools? In many districts, the majority of households do not have children attending public schools. Parents need the support of nonparents who see the value of supporting their local school system.

Are there community events that encourage families to partici-pate together? If you are planning community celebrations, orga-nize events that will naturally draw families together. Host ice cream socials, youth-adult talent shows, or age-appropriate movie showings in a local park at dusk.

If your city provides information packets for neighborhoods organizing block parties, be sure there are suggestions for intergenerational activities that can bring families together and help them get to know one another.

Is your community becoming more ethnically diverse? Work with your local library or an English Language Learner program to create displays celebrating all types of families. Ask families to share recipes, pictures, and favorite family stories as part of the display.

LET THESE REAL-LIFE EXAMPLES INSPIRE CHANGE IN YOUR COMMUNITY!

- Merchants in a number of communities designate parking spots near the door as reserved for mothers-to-be or mothers of infants and toddlers.

- When Colebrook Associates, a group of community volunteers in Colebrook, Connecticut, hears of a resident who's having trouble paying bills or buying gas, it mails checks to utility companies or donates prepaid gasoline cards.

- A florist in St. Louis Park, Minnesota, provides flowers to all the children in a local housing complex so they all have a gift for their moms on Mother's Day.

- As a community member you will spot many opportunities to support families. Find ways to draw on your own special interests or talents to make your community supportive of parents and their families.

Going Further as a Caring Adult to Families

Think about the families you know. All families go through significant challenges to their personal limits and abilities, whether it is parents dealing with their own aging parents, coping with a family illness, losing a job or dealing with debt, or struggling with the occasionally wrenching emotional ups and downs of everyday life. If you know a family that is going through a challenging time, think creatively about ways you can help them spend some relaxed time with each other. Deliver a movie and a package of popcorn to them for a movie night, or invite them all over for dinner. Offer to babysit younger children or help care for an elderly relative who's living with them. It might be that telling parents something positive about their child is just what they need, or perhaps you can offer a listening ear so a parent can share concerns and come to a new perspective.

When you see parents in your neighborhood, make an effort to tell them something positive about their children. If you tell them how diligently their teenager has been working on perfecting his pitching, or how thankful you are for their child's help in raking your leaves, it will encourage them to express their own appreciation to their children. Children need their parents to encourage them to do their best and tell them they have the skills, talents, and follow-through to achieve what they set out to do.

ACTIVITY 1

Define It!

You will need:

- Easel
- Markers
- Newsprint or butcher paper
- Pencils or pens
- Writing paper

Focus: Youth create a definition of *family*.

Set the stage: Begin by asking each young person to write a one-sentence definition of *family*. After a few minutes, ask the group to brainstorm words that describe families. Remember to accept all suggestions without comment, and record each one on newsprint.

Step 1: Form teams of three. Challenge each team to create and agree on a one-sentence definition of family, based on their individual work and the ideas generated during the group brainstorm. Each team should write its definition on newsprint.

Step 2: Post the definitions from the teams, allowing a few minutes for each team to explain its thinking and answer questions about its work. (Note: Be sensitive to those who have challenging family situations or who draft a definition that seems bleak or disturbing. As an alternative, ask group members to comment on the kind of family that they hope to create as adults.)

Step 3: Note similarities and differences in the definitions. Then ask:

- What do families need in order for everyone to be healthy and safe? (For example, money, food, shelter, health care.)
- What do families need to stay emotionally healthy? (For example, talking to each other, being honest, showing support.)
- What other kinds of support do families provide?
- What is your definition of a high quality of life as an adult? (For example, being happy, having a good job, making a difference.) Is family part of that dream?
- If you or another young person is not receiving enough family support, what can be done to get more support? How can friends help?

This activity originally appeared in Rebecca Grothe, More Building Assets Together *(Search Institute, 2002).*

ACTIVITY 2

Family Photo Fair

Focus: Youth recall times when they have been supported and loved.

Before the group arrives: Ask each youth to bring one or two favorite family photos, with each photo showing at least two people. Or suggest that youth bring in a picture of someone they think of as "family" (someone who has been supportive, but is not necessarily related). Be sure to bring your own favorite photos as well. It may take several sessions to collect all the pictures.

Set the stage: Have each person show her or his photos to the group, answering these questions:

- Who are the people shown?
- When and where was the picture taken?
- What happened immediately before the photo was taken? What happened after it was taken?
- What were the people talking about before the photo was taken?

After all group members have shown their photos, spend some time discussing the following questions:

- What surprised you the most in these stories?
- What did your experiences have in common? How were your experiences different?
- What are some ways that your families give you support, love, and encouragement?
- How do you support, love, and encourage others in your family?

This activity originally appeared in Rebecca Grothe, More Building Assets Together *(Search Institute, 2002).*

2

POSITIVE FAMILY COMMUNICATION

Young person and her or his parents(s) communicate positively, and young person is willing to seek advice and counsel from parents.

Twenty-eight percent of youth in grades 6 through 12 reported experiencing this asset in their lives.

This information is based on data collected on 148,189 students surveyed in 2003 using *Search Institute Profiles of Student Life: Attitudes and Behaviors.*

Positive family communication is an important part of a young person's development. It includes opportunities to talk and a willingness to listen to each other. Expressing opinions and having discussions with their parents allows youth to build their sense of identity and to explore their values.

While 68 percent of young people believe their family loves and supports them (Asset 1: Family Support), only 28 percent say they experience Positive Family Communication (Asset 2) and are willing to seek advice or counsel from their parents.

In My Family

All parents have times when they fall short in communicating with their child. Maybe they are distracted by a difficult day at work or they are caught off guard by a challenging question. Parents are often trying to do three things at once and suddenly realize they haven't been following what their child has been trying to tell them.

One way you can get better at building the Positive Family Communication asset is to reflect on it, examine how you are currently trying to build it, and push yourself to identify ways you could become even more intentional about building it.

Ask yourself the following questions:

- What was communication like in your family when you were growing up? How do you remember communicating with your parents most of the time? How do you remember them communicating with you?

- What is one example of a time when you know you were really listened to and heard by one of your parents? What made you feel that way?

- What is an example of a time when you felt misunderstood or dismissed by one of your parents? What made you feel that way?

- How might your answers to these questions influence your interactions with children and teens now? For example, if you often felt disappointed by your own parents' poor communication skills, do you now make a special point of listening to your own children and making time for extended conversations?

In a gathering of parents who were asked these questions, one father said, "In my family, being a good debater was the way to get attention. Family dinners would get louder and louder as everyone jockeyed to be sure they got their point in. Now that I have children of my own, I'm trying hard to pause and really listen to what they are saying, instead of jumping in to counter their point with one of my own. I really have to work at remembering that conversations are not about racking up points."

A mother commented that in her family, people didn't really talk about what they were feeling. "We used to watch to see if our dad was clenching his jaw—that was how we could tell if we were upsetting him."

Another mother said, "I was really shy when I was a child. My mom always had a snack for me after school, and she would ask me to describe something interesting I had learned that day. Sometimes that would be the first time I had opened my mouth all day. There were days when I felt like she was just being nosey, but I realize now that she was helping me find my voice."

An important finding out of developmental psychology research that is described in *Developmental Assets: A Synthesis of the Scientific Research on Adolescent Development*[5] is that parent-child interactions are two-way. Not only do parents have an effect on their adolescent's behavior, but an adolescent's behavior has an impact on her or his parent's behavior, setting up a cycle of either positive or negative communication and relatedness.[6] Also, when adolescents are open to parents' influence, the parents feel more capable. Parents who have made an effort to improve family relations have reported that receiving a positive response from their children made it easier to keep trying.

If you are not a parent, you can put this information to good use by praising parents and reinforcing the positive ways they interact with their children. It will give them a boost of confidence, thereby encouraging a cycle of healthy communication.

How Do I Resolve *This* Issue?

Most parents run into situations in which they aren't sure what to do. Fortunately, parents have all sorts of resources available to them, and many are on topics related to family communication. School districts often sponsor parent education classes or one-time speakers. These may be offered through the Community Education office. Some are sponsored by the local parent-teacher association. In addition, many other organizations, from congregations to local university extension offices and nonprofits serving families, have an array of programs and services designed to give parents strategies they can use to improve their parenting skills. Libraries and bookstores can suggest books that are age-specific or geared toward certain issues. Your local librarian can also help you find other local resources.

Parents who learn to take a strength-based approach when communicating with their children or teens often find their conversations are less adversarial and more oriented toward mutual problem solving. For examples of these kinds of conversations see *Parenting at the Speed of Teens* (Search Institute, 2004).

Learning positive communication skills not only will benefit you as a parent but also will give your child skills he or she can carry into future relationships.

> I've known about the assets for a long time, and I've always been struck by how few young people experience Positive Family Communication [28 percent] yet how many claim to experience Family Support [68 percent]. I've asked several teens about that, and my impression is that even when communication is rocky, they want and need to believe their family is loving and supportive—and they can sense that love, even when the communication hits a snag. To me it says they are always willing to give us another chance to get it right. —*Mother of two and school volunteer*

Building Positive Family Communication One-on-One

Part of my interest in writing this book stems from all that I have learned as a parent of two boys. They have taught me a lot about the Support assets and have let me know that while sometimes my parenting was right on target, sometimes it was way off. I actually thought I was a great mom, until my oldest son turned 13. Then it seemed as if we were always butting heads. One day I said to him, "David, I miss the great conversations we used to have." He turned to me and said, "I do too, Mom, but that was when I was a little kid and you had to protect me all the time. Now I'm not a little kid, and I don't like it when you comment on every choice I make. You have to trust me and start letting go." And I realized he was right—that what worked when he was 6 was not going to work now that he was 13, and I had to make some big changes in how I communicated with him about the choices he was making and in how I set boundaries with him. Over time we moved to a new place where we could start having great conversations again, but it took us time to figure out how to make that happen.

GETTING STARTED

Let's look at where you are right now in terms of family communication. Wherever you are, there are easy ways to make improvements. Take a few moments to think about the following statements.

	Frequently	Sometimes	Rarely	Never
My child asks for my advice.				
I have in-depth conversations with my child on a variety of topics.				
I make myself available to my child when she wants to talk.				
I really listen to what my child has to say.				

Find a quiet time when you and your child can sit down together. Tell her that having good family communication is important to you and that you want her feedback on how she thinks things are going. Ask her the following questions, and encourage complete honesty:

- How often do you ask me for advice?

- Do you think we have in-depth conversations on a variety of topics?

- Am I usually available to listen when you want to talk?

- Do you think I *really* listen to what you have to say?

Compare your child's answers to what you marked in the grid you completed. Tell her you care about her and want to work on family communication. Ask her what one change you could make to improve communication between the two of you. If she's stuck for an answer, remind her of the questions you asked and the answers she gave. For example, if she doesn't think you're *really* listening to her, prompt her to explain why she feels that way. Is it your body language or eye contact? Is it how you respond? Is it whether you follow up on conversations that are important to her?

Take a deep breath before you respond to her answers, particularly if she has touched on a sensitive spot. Showing our children that we're not perfect but that we want to improve because we love them is one of the most powerful things we can share with them. Acting on our promises is another. Remember to follow up on this conversation and make a daily effort to work on any weak areas of communication.

STRIKING UP A CONVERSATION WITH YOUR CHILD

Many of the most meaningful conversations children have with their parents happen during those unscheduled moments when they're just "hanging out." Here are some good starting points:

Make yourself available for conversations. Notice whether your children are hanging around you—it is often a signal that they want to talk.

Help them start the conversation. With some children, it is enough to ask, "Is there something you'd like to talk about?" With other children, or for highly charged topics, it can help to invite them to do a routine task with you, which gives them a way to begin the conversation without feeling as though they have a spotlight on them. Folding laundry, washing dishes, cooking, working in the garden—any shared task can create a comfort zone for conversation. Remember, too, that time together in a car can be a great way to get a conversation in.

One young woman fondly remembers family road trips as opportunities to bond with her father. At night, she got to sit in the front with her dad while her mother sat in the back to get her sister to sleep. As everyone else drifted off and the stars came out, she and her dad would talk about what he was like when he was her age and how he had dealt with problems like the ones she was facing.

Really listen for what your child is trying to say. Sometimes young people feel something very deeply, but they may have trouble expressing those feelings in words. Giving them time to figure out how to express themselves helps them get in touch with their emotions.

Find ways to connect every day. Make family mealtimes a priority. Studies point out that children who eat with their families on a regular basis do better in school and are better able to resist a host of risk behaviors. If everyone scatters to evening events, meet over breakfast instead of dinner or create a weekend brunch tradition.

Create some conversational routines. One family's members talk about the best thing they saw or experienced that day. Another has a book of questions that someone opens at random and each member of the family takes a turn responding. See Mary Ackerman, *Conversations on the Go: Clever Questions to Keep Teens and Grown-Ups Talking* (Search Institute, 2004), for sample questions.

Work on strategies to get past conversational dead ends. How familiar is the following example of an after-school conversation?

"Do you have any homework?"
"No."
"How did you do on your test?"
"Fine."

Ask unique questions that discourage one-word answers, such as, "What was the strongest emotion you felt today? Do you know what triggered that emotion?" Direct requests work, too: "Teach me about something you learned today."

Tell your child every day that you love him. Parents often assume that their children know this, but actually hearing the words makes a tremendous difference.

If there are other adults in your home, model open communication with them.

Not all the communication you have with your child has to happen one-on-one. There are additional ways you can create settings that allow for positive communication between you and your child:

Start a parent-child book club with several of your child's friends and their parents. One group of mothers and daughters in St. Louis Park, Minnesota, started a book club when the girls were in grade 5. The gatherings provided an opportunity to deepen friendships among the girls and among the mothers, while also surrounding each girl with a circle of strong women who encouraged her to "find her voice" through the book club discussions and general conversations. If you aren't sure what books to pick, your local librarian or your child's school librarian will be happy to identify books that both youth and adults will find interesting for a book club discussion. Some local bookstore chains have also developed discussion guides for various types of book clubs, and many books now include such questions as an aid to book group members.

Participate in groups that support parent-child events, such as Girl Scouts, Boy Scouts, Camp Fire, YMCA, or YWCA.

In My Professional Life

Sometimes the most helpful way caring adults can remind young people that their parents care about them is to help them tackle difficult conversations. If teens in your program or at your workplace often talk about how unfair their latest curfew, driving restriction, or homework rule is, you can acknowledge their frustration, and say that even though it may not seem like it right now, their parents must really care about them to put those rules in place. Sometimes just allowing young people to vent their frustrations helps them come around and see the love behind the restriction.

There may be times when you find yourself in a deep conversation with a young person, or a teen you know might drop a hint that something serious is on her or his mind. In either case, encouraging these young people to talk with their parents is a good course of action. Let them practice an opening line or two on you. Offer your feedback, and encourage them to find a good time to begin the conversation (e.g., after a family dinner, not when everyone is rushing out the door in the morning). They will go in better prepared and leave with more fulfilling results. Let them know they can always talk with you after they have spoken with their parents.

There are many simple but powerful ways you can foster this asset in families:

Get to know the names of the young people's parents. If you already know a young person's parent, communicate something specific and positive about the parent to the young person. Sometimes getting someone else's perspective on her or his parents can help a young person look at them from another vantage point.

Find occasions to tell their parents what a great kid they have. Naming some small, specific thing their child has done makes it real, and creates an opportunity for a conversation between parent and child.

Find opportunities to help young people develop their communications skills. They will be able to use these skills at home and in other settings.

Encourage young people to share a particular activity with their parents so they can discuss it at home or do the activity together.

Create opportunities for young people to put on skits about daily living situations, where one has to play the role of parent. This will put them in their parents' shoes as they act out what they would do if they were the parent. Homework, dating, bedtimes, curfews, and driving are just a few themes that can form the basis for a skit. Young people can suggest others that are relevant to them.

What's My Place?

Some young people live in families that rarely use positive communication. Some youth experience yelling, name-calling, insults, and even physical abuse. How do you address these issues? One mentor made a point of inviting her family to spend time with her mentee. As she interacted with her husband and children, she modeled positive communication. Later she explained to her mentee how important it is to be patient, loving, and respectful to family members. The mentor described her own mother's poor communication skills. She told her mentee, "I can't control my mother's behavior, but *I* can choose to communicate positively."

Reaching Out to Parents

If you work with youth, you most likely know many parents in addition to the parents of the youth in your class or program. These might be people you work with, parents of your children's friends, or parents you know in your neighborhood or congregation. You can help other parents by sharing what you know about the Developmental Assets and asset building. You can also post flyers about various parent resources and programs that are available in your area.

Talk with parents about your successes and failures in conversations with young people. All parents lose their cool sometimes, and it's comforting for them to know they're not alone.

Gather a group of parents to share their best experiences. When did they communicate well? What did these positive experiences have in common? One parent may offer helpful advice about having a serious talk about sex, and another may be skilled at negotiating fair consequences for misbehavior.

In My Community

There are many ways you can reach out to fellow community members who could use some support. Even if you are not a teacher or parenting professional, you can still provide much-needed (and much-appreciated) help to parents in your community.

If you are a parent, donate the parenting books and resources you have found helpful to your local library.

Volunteer to teach a class with an emphasis on parenting. You don't have to be an expert on the subject—classes that bring families together for a fun time will also help them communicate better. Maybe your favorite hobby is scrapbooking—how about leading a parent-child course? Are you or your child skilled with computers? Perhaps the two of you can team-teach. Not only will you be teaching people a valuable new skill, you will also be modeling positive family communication as you're building this asset with your own child.

If you volunteer as a coach, set some ground rules at the beginning of a season about the ways parents can provide positive support for their children and others who are participating. In this era of parents starting fights with other parents at their children's sporting events, naming appropriate behavior will help establish what is expected. Just as some sports leagues have created an athletes' code of conduct, you can create a parents' code of conduct, and share reasons why this positive communication is important for the healthy development of all young people participating in the sport.

Talk to your local hospital. In New Richmond, Wisconsin, all new mothers receive a set of eight cardboard building blocks with the eight asset categories attached to them, and a list of the 40 assets when they leave the maternity ward. High school students help assemble the packets.

Pediatricians are always looking for resources that they can share with parents. Have a conversation with local doctors about the Developmental Assets and ask if they would be willing to display a poster or make printed resources available for families.

If you own a business, contact local parent education groups and offer to hang flyers about their parenting courses in your break room or another spot where employees can see them.

Talk to your school district or library about hosting an intergenerational conversation on local issues affecting youth. Encourage youth to invite their parents.

Find out whether your faith community offers any activities centered on families or parenting. Encourage leaders to do so. Another place to start is to include children and teens during "coffee hour" or invite parents and children to serve together as "greeters," or propose service projects that parents and their children can participate in together.

Watch your community's paper for stories about healthy families. If all the news about families tends toward the sensational and the negative, write a letter to the editor encouraging more balanced coverage to include some of the positive activities families are engaged in. Invite local families to write an opinion piece about the important strengths families bring to their communities.

ACTIVITY 1

What's My Line?

You will need:

- 3 × 5 index cards or a sheet of paper
- scissors

Focus: Students discuss how to communicate with their parents or guardians.

Before the group arrives: Write each of the following situations on a 3 × 5 card or type the situations on a sheet of paper and cut them apart:

- Your parent says you have to be home by 10:00 p.m.
- Your parent promises to be at an important event but never shows up.
- Your parent interrupts you while you are on a phone call and asks you to take out the garbage.
- Your parent forgets to sign a permission slip, and you miss a fun field trip.
- You are about to head out to a party. Your parent asks you whom you are going with, where you plan to be, and whether an adult will be present.
- You had a hard day at school and when you get home your parent tells you you have to babysit your two younger siblings for three hours.
- You observe your parent drinking too much.
- Your parent has received your report card and focuses on the one grade that could be better, instead of commenting on other positive grades.

Begin by discussing how conflicts can escalate or be resolved depending on how each person in the conflict chooses to communicate. Ask for a few examples.

Assign youth to small groups. Have each group select a situation card, and then instruct the groups to write two versions of a short skit using the situation card as the starting point. Invite them to write one skit in which their response is an example of poor communication in action, and one skit that presents a parent and teen trying to work things through together.

Have students act out their skits for the other groups, and then ask them to discuss examples they saw in the skits of both good and not-so-good communication strategies.

After one run-through, encourage teens in the "audience" to suggest alternatives they could choose in response to a parent's initial statement on a particular topic.

Ask everyone what they learned from watching the skits. Ask which strategies they think they could use. (Secondary questions: Was it easy or hard to play the part of the parent? Was it easy or hard to play the part of a child escalating the conflict? De-escalating the conflict?)

ACTIVITY 2

Tough Topics

You will need:
- paper or stationery
- pens or pencils

Focus: Young people brainstorm ways to approach difficult subjects with their parents.

Most youth (and their parents) have at least one or two topics that they find difficult to discuss. Ask the group if there are any conversations they've been avoiding with their parents. If they feel comfortable doing so, have them name these topics. Chances are good that many youth will name the same things, such as sex, dating, or drug use.

Ask the teens if they've tried to strike up any of these conversations with their parents, and how they went about it. If they hit a dead end, ask them why they think that happened and if they have any ideas about how to try again.

Mention that a constructive way to work through thoughts and feelings is to write them down. Suggest that they each write a letter to their parent, naming the topic and why they wish they could talk about it with their parent. If you have time and the teens feel comfortable, have them start their letters (emphasize that no one else will read them) so you can discuss the activity as a group. Give the group about 10 minutes.

Now ask them how writing the letters made them feel. Let them know they can give the letter to their parent, but it's not necessary to do so. The point of the exercise is to get their thoughts on paper and encourage them to sit down with their parents to talk. Ask them to imagine the response they might get if they do give the letter to their parents. If they don't think they would get a positive or receptive response, encourage them to approach another adult in their life with whom they would be comfortable discussing that topic.

OTHER ADULT RELATIONSHIPS

Young person receives support from three or more nonparent adults.

Forty-three percent of youth in grades 6 through 12 report experiencing this asset in their lives.

This information is based on data collected on 148,189 students surveyed in 2003 using *Search Institute Profiles of Student Life: Attitudes and Behaviors*.

All young people need to have a sense that they are known, and that all adults, not just their parents, care about them. Pick up any memoir about a successful leader and you will find stories about the adults from the person's youth who influenced the way she thought about herself, her future, and who she became. But just under two-thirds of youth in grades 4 through 6 and fewer than half of all youth in grades 6 through 12 feel the presence of three or more "other caring adults" in their lives.

By picking up *this* book you have already taken a first step toward building strong relationships with young people. Far too many adults today believe that raising children is someone else's job. But families and schools cannot do the work alone.

In My Family

It may seem odd to think that one of your jobs as a parent is to help your children connect to caring adults outside the family. As parents we would like to think we can provide all the love and attention our children need. But the reality is that we can't do it alone. Children and teens need care from their parents, but they also need to be seen and appreciated by and connected to other caring adults who can expand their horizons, teach them new skills, and encourage them to try new things.

Stranger Danger

As parents we may have another reason we are reluctant to think about this asset of Other Adult Relationships. With news stories about abductions and missing children's faces staring out at us from milk cartons and mailers, it is not surprising that our first impulse is to protect our children from other adults. But for the sake of our children's healthy development, we have to stretch beyond that first impulse. In fact, according to the National Center for Missing and Exploited Children, in 2001 about 99 percent of missing children were found within hours or days.[7]

Keep in mind that many caring adults have heard the same news stories and looked at the same milk cartons, and may be reluctant to engage with young people, fearing their interest will be misinterpreted. Parents can help clear this hurdle by thinking about adults within their circle of friends who might be willing to connect with a youth if offered a direct invitation.

What might such an invitation sound like?

My daughter is trying out for her first play next month. I know you performed in theater productions in high school. Would you be willing to talk to her about how to get ready for her audition? I know she'd really appreciate some advice from someone who's been there.

My son is trying to come up with a service project he and his church group can do. Haven't you volunteered with Habitat for Humanity and a local food shelf? Would you be willing to chat with him about your experiences with those two organizations and what kinds of projects he might be able to do?

My son and I are getting on each other's nerves right now, and I think he needs to talk to someone outside the family. Would you be willing to spend an hour with him at a coffee shop sometime this week? He has said he thinks you're cool, and I know what a good listener you are. I don't expect you to come back and report on the conversation. I just want him to have someone trustworthy to talk to.

You can also ask your child to name adults outside the family that she feels she can trust, or that she admires. You can help her start a conversation with one of these caring adults, and you can support her in developing friendships with them. With younger children, it can be appropriate to contact the adult and thank them for showing an interest in your child.

In My Professional Life

Sometimes working with young people can be overwhelming. No matter how much you care about them, you may feel that you can't provide everything they need. The good news is that you don't have to. It is better for young people to have multiple caring adults in their lives, so one way you can support them is by helping them connect with other caring adults. How might you do this? Think about the staff in your building. Think beyond program delivery staff. Many youth centers and YMCAs have trained all employees, including custodians and front desk staff, to be intentional about building Developmental Assets. Everyone is encouraged to learn the names of the young people in the building and to greet them by name. Young people gravitate toward adults who seem to show a genuine concern and perhaps have a shared interest. Staff throughout your building can play a role as caring adults, and you can facilitate this by offering training so they understand the important role they can play in the lives of young people in your building.

Do you include service projects as a part of your activities? Think about the places in your community where young people can connect with other adults. Some communities have chore services organized by the local United Way or by a social service agency. Community members, including young people, can sign up to rake leaves, change storm windows, or do other chores that help elderly or disabled residents stay in their homes. If you participate in these chore services, be sure to make time for the young people to meet and talk with the adult living there.

If your group visits a local nursing home, think in advance about the project you're going to do. Will it maximize the opportunities young people have to connect with the residents? You may decide that a weekly or monthly trip to play cards or work on jigsaw puzzles or crafts offers more opportunities for friendship building than a one-time event. Relationships take time to develop, so think about how you can ensure enough time for those opportunities to emerge.

STORIES OF SUPPORT

When I was growing up, I loved to read. The trip to the local library was a highlight. Mrs. Homan was our children's librarian. When I would come down the big stone stairs, she would say, "Laura, it is so great to see you. I have a special book just for you." Sometimes she would pull the book right out of her drawer as if she were saving it for me. When I was in the 2nd or 3rd grade, most of my friends were reading the Little House series. I was just not interested. It was a little too difficult for me. Instead, I was hooked on the Carolyn Haywood books—B Is for Betsy. My mom was concerned that they were too easy and approached Mrs. Homan about it. Mrs. Homan reassured her that it was more important that I was enjoying reading than reading the harder books. Not only was Mrs. Homan a support to me but also to our family. My mom and I both agree that her support of my reading and also her advice not to push me really influenced not only my love of reading but also to this day I have good comprehension and great speed. —Laura Meverden, program director, YMCA, Appleton, Wisconsin

Being That Special Someone

Every one of us has opportunities to play a role in building the Other Adult Relationships asset for the young people whose paths we cross. Think of a young person's life as a weaving on a loom. There are the long warp threads that form the frame on which the weaving takes place. Some of these threads are created by the young person alone.

Some are created by family members and friends of all ages who are present over many years in the life of that young person. Weaving in and out of these threads are the many colors that make the pattern in that life. You, as a caring adult, might be a major part of the overall design that emerges, or your particular color might be a bright accent that plays a small supporting role in building the overall design.

Barbara Bridgwater, Community Youth Champion with Youth Count in Indiana, remembers a caring adult from her high school years, Alice Mary Ranck Hettle, her Latin teacher.

"The first time I met Miss Ranck was on my first day of Latin class. She did not walk into the room, she marched into the room with more energy and enthusiasm than I've ever seen from another individual."

For the next three years, Miss Ranck provided constant support and encouragement. She challenged her students to accomplish their goals, and was open to what success meant to each young person. "Nothing but a student's best would meet her expectations," Barbara says. "If the best was a C+, then that was fine, but if a student was capable of an A- or an A+, then that's what the student needed to produce."

But Miss Ranck's positive influence didn't end with high school graduation. She continued to be supportive of Barbara into her adulthood. In fact, Miss Ranck continued to be a caring person in the lives of many of her former students, including many of Barbara's relatives—so much so that she even attended their family reunion.

"I've carried her lessons with me these many years," Barbara says.

If you work with young people, you have many opportunities to be a caring adult in the lives of the children or teens in your program. Although you may be pressured to focus on measurable outcomes, it is important to remember that the relationships you form with young people are at least as important as the content you are trying to cover in your program. In fact, teachers and program providers have said over and over that the time spent at the outset on building relationships makes everything about program delivery go more smoothly.

Think about how you create a safe environment with the students in your group. Do you have them generate rules they want to follow while they are in your program? Do you reinforce kindness among the young people in your program? Can you occasionally set aside your lesson plan to deal with a pressing issue that has agitated or excited the group? In other words, do you show them by your actions that you are attentive to their needs?

Whether you're a teacher, mentor, or counselor who works directly with young people on a daily basis, or a customer at a young person's after-school job or a friendly neighbor who has occasional but meaningful interactions with young people, you have what it takes to be a very special part of a young person's life. Not only will you make a young person's life better, your own life will become richer and more rewarding, and you will be contributing to a warmer environment for us all.

CHECKUP

Think about the young people with whom you work. Which two do you know the best? Why? Which two do you know the least? What can you do in the next week to get to know those two young people better?

At the end of the week ask yourself: What unique skill or strength or attribute did I discover about the two young people I set out to get to know better this week?

Fill the Gap

A great way to put this asset into action is to be aware of what is going on in a young person's life. Have you noticed that one teenager often needs a ride to school or work? Offer to give him a ride home now and then, or help him find a bus schedule or carpool he can join.

Is he often unprepared or short on needed supplies? Ask him if his parent(s) are able to provide the supplies, and try to find the root of the problem. Is it an issue of money, or are the parent(s) often absent so the young person has no one to take him shopping? Does he feel uncomfortable telling his parent(s) that he needs something for school, work, or extracurricular activities?

Can you remember the last time you saw his parent(s) at an important event? Make a point of showing up to games, plays, or concerts. Whenever you can, try to be that missing link in a young person's life.

Young people aren't the only ones who can benefit from the presence of other caring adults. Parents can, too. While it is important that parents make a point of attending their children's events and being there on special occasions, it is not always possible. Alison's mother, Mary, had a commitment she couldn't get out of on the day of Alison's senior prom. So Mary enlisted the support of a neighbor they both knew well, and that woman helped Alison get dressed and took pictures. She fussed over Alison as much as Mary would have—she tugged at her dress, helped her with her makeup, and made sure she took several pictures of Alison and her date.

Everyone involved benefited from the arrangement. Instead of being racked with guilt because she couldn't be in two places at one time, Mary was able to fulfill her commitment and still managed to see Alison off to the prom. Alison knew there was another adult in her life who cared about her very much, so she was able to enjoy herself while she was getting ready for a big night. Their neighbor was delighted to be there for her young friend—she had seen her grow up, so it was a special experience for her as well.

In My Community

Young people receive feedback about their worth every day as they move around in their communities. A young person may be told to put his backpack by the door in a convenience store while an older woman with a large shopping bag is allowed in without comment. Billboards and bus stop ads portray teens as a separate and difficult-to-understand species. The media report on teen crime. Rarely do young people hear or see themselves recognized for their volunteer work, their passion for social causes, or the many large and small ways they contribute to their families, schools, and communities. Young people need us to recognize and name their unique strengths and qualities. They need to know we see them as individuals, not as a part of a generic peer group called "teens."

If you regularly cross paths with a young person in a store or other public space, start by adding a smile and eye contact along with your usual "thank you." Work your way up to adding another sentence.

Before you know it, you may be having a conversation. Don't give up if you don't get an immediate response. Try a few more times to see if the young person shows interest in a longer conversation. When a roomful of adults was asked how they started a conversation with a teenager they didn't know, here were some of their conversation starters:

- "I see you're studying calculus. I really struggled with that."

- "I love that shade of blue [red, green, violet] hair color. How long does it last?"

- "Thanks for remembering how I like my coffee. How do you keep us all straight?"

- [If they are wearing a school team shirt] "I see you're on the [soccer, basketball, track] team. How's the season going?"

If you are part of a faith community, don't forget opportunities to start a conversation with young people you see at your church, synagogue, mosque, or other gathering place. If you are on a committee, ask if a young person or two can be added to the group. If there are young people there, make a point of thanking them and chatting with them before or after meetings. *Really* listen to them, and show that you value their input in committee meetings. Model this for the other adults who are involved—young people can't feel truly supported if they feel they are the token youth member of a committee.

What's My Place?

Sometimes we observe family situations that seem unhealthy, and we may find ourselves wanting to step in to help the children involved or to give the parents advice. In many cases, however, we need to refrain from crossing boundaries. Unless a child is in danger, it is often best to respect the family's privacy and parenting methods. So how can we help build assets for children in these situations? We can be very intentional about becoming a caring adult and letting them know they are always welcome to come to us.

One Minneapolis woman experienced a situation similar to this when she lived in a duplex. The three little girls who lived in the unit above her often seemed to be lonely and in need of attention. The woman had limited opportunities to interact with the children, so she made a point of smiling and waving whenever she could.

One day the girls told her they couldn't use their basketball because they weren't allowed to play outside. She felt terrible.

"A million little ideas ran through my head, like maybe I could buy them a Nerf indoor basketball set! But I knew it wouldn't be right for me to buy them something."

Instead, she made a point of trying to engage the girls in conversations. She finally got them to open up about their Halloween costumes. Their faces lit up when they talked about dressing up—they said it was one of their favorite things to do.

"Once I found that out, I went through my jewelry box and found several necklaces and bracelets I never wore, and I dug through a storage chest and found four old purses. I told the girls they could have this stuff to play dress-up. They were so excited! It was a small gesture, but they always seemed to be craving attention, and I think my taking an interest in them made them feel special."

> "We live in a world in which we need to share responsibility. It's easy to say 'It's not my child, not my community, not my world, not my problem.' Then there are those who see the need and respond. I consider those people my heroes." —Fred Rogers, *Mister Rogers' Neighborhood*

Make a pact with yourself to get to know one of the young people in *your* neighborhood. In this era of "stranger danger," many young people and their parents are anxious about adults they don't know. Start slowly by introducing yourself to parents. As you begin to earn trust, mention that you have been reading about how important other adults are in the lives of young people. Explain to parents that you would like to get to know a few more young people in your neighborhood as part of being a good neighbor.

Dear Search Institute:

This should be a happy letter for you to read because it describes a success story. It all started a few years ago when our circuit court judge invited one of your eloquent speakers to come to Richland County and enlighten us. I was an unsuspecting member of the audience.

Afterward, I decided to try asset building in my own rural, isolated valley, inhabited by a few active farm families and three or four nonfarming households.

Accustomed to walking for exercise every early morning, I started to time my walks to coincide with the arrival of the school bus picking up the neighborhood kids. Before long, I knew all four children by name, they knew me, and we had a pleasant exchange of small talk and body language.

When I started looking to expand the asset building, I hit upon the idea of attending the local high school varsity soccer games. Soccer was the only game I knew because I grew up in Holland, where football and baseball were unknown. To my surprise, I discovered that only family members of players attended the games. I was the only nonfamily member on the bleachers. To this day, four years later, that is still the case.

But being the only "outside" fan brought unique advantages for asset building because, before long, I got to know all 18 families on the benches, and through them, all 18 members of the team. Now, whenever I go shopping in our small town, a current or past soccer player invariably changes my oil, checks my groceries, or waves at me while mowing the right-of-way. I have been invited to graduation parties and notified of hospitalizations or successful college entrances. I really got to know a lot of teenagers, and they got to know me. Assets were being built en masse while having fun.

Last night was the night of the annual soccer banquet. As usual, I was the only nonfamily member enjoying the accolades the soccer players received from their coaches and the generous applause from their parents and grandparents. At the end of the evening, the player who had received the highest award was asked to say a few words. He hesitantly rose, straightened himself, and said, "I want to thank Henk for coming to all our games. It meant a lot to me."

I was moved. Driving home, I realized how much this statement meant to me and how it all started with learning about asset building.

From the bottom of my heart, thanks.

Henk Newenhouse
Lone Rock, Wisconsin

Greet kids when they're outside on their bikes or walking home from the bus stop. Be kind and gracious when kids come to your door trying to sell items for their school fund-raisers. Ask them if they're raising money for a specific cause, and if they're selling candy bars or magazines, ask if they have any recommendations. As you befriend young neighbors, try any of the following starting points:

Talk about your own children, if you have any—or nieces, nephews, or mentees—and their interests, especially if you have noticed common interests. Maybe your children are older and would be good informal coaches or teachers to a younger kid in the neighborhood.

Share a story about yourself as a young person and something you were interested in, or a neighbor who took an interest in you.

Ask about their interests, and follow up! Remember what you've talked about so you can take the conversation further the next time you run into each other.

Invite a young person to help you with your garden or cook with you, if those are activities you would enjoy sharing. Make sure he asks his parents, and perhaps invite the parents as well.

Hire a teen to pet-sit your animals, water your plants, or take in your mail while you're away on vacation.

Comment on any shared interests. If you see them getting in the car with soccer balls or hockey sticks or basketballs, and you share an interest in that sport, ask about their team. Attend a game if they seem to respond to your comments.

If sports aren't your area of interest, attend your local school's music concerts or theatrical productions. Volunteer to help behind the scenes or on event nights. Theater groups are often thrilled to receive assistance from someone who can help make or find costumes or assist a set crew using power tools for the first time.

It's important that parents feel they know you as well in order to trust that your intentions are appropriate for their child. Extend your asset-building neighborliness to parents as well as kids.

Creating a caring neighborhood is more than being there for youth—work to create a strong, supportive network so all members of your neighborhood are tight-knit.

Whom Do You Go To?

You will need:

- seven sheets of newsprint
- a marker

Focus: Youth identify whom they would turn to for advice in a variety of situations.

Make seven newsprint signs labeled "Neighbor," "Boss," "Activity Director or Coach," "Extended Family," "Teacher," "Other Adult," and "No Other Adult." Space the signs around the room. Then have youth stand in the middle.

Explain that you're going to name different situations, and youth should go to the sign that reflects whom they'd go to for advice on that issue. Explain that "Extended Family" could refer to any adult in their extended family: grandparents, uncles, aunts, adult cousins, or other relative. Tell youth to choose "Other Adult" for the other adults and to choose "No Other Adult" when they feel they wouldn't go to anyone listed.

Name issues or situations such as the following, allowing time for youth to get to the appropriate sign each time:

- Just to talk
- To talk about dating and relationships
- What to do after graduation
- Getting into trouble with the police
- If you or a friend got pregnant or got someone pregnant
- Just to hang out with
- Borrowing money
- Questions about alcohol or other drugs
- Getting a bad grade
- Figuring out where you stand on an issue

Once you finish, ask:

- Which adults outside of your family do you go to most often for advice and support? Why? Least often? Why?

- What keeps you from going to some people?
- How do you feel about the number of adult supports you have outside your family?
- Who else can you think of who could give you support?

This activity originally appeared in Jolene L. Roehlkepartain, Building Assets Together *(Minneapolis, 1997).*

ACTIVITY 2

Long-Distance Support

You will need:

- markers
- newsprint
- writing paper

Focus: Youth produce a list of ways to keep in touch with those in their support network.

Set the stage: Introduce the focus of this activity by asking youth to share the names of people who support and care for them even though they don't see them very often (twice a month or less). Ask:

- How do you know these people care about you even though you are not together in the same place very often?
- Are there people whom you support, even though you aren't with them very often? How do you do this?

Step 1: Form teams of three or four. Announce that in each team the youth sitting closest to the door will be the recorder and the one who is the oldest will be the timekeeper. Tell groups that their assignment is to come up with as many ideas as possible for keeping in touch with supporters who are not with us often. They will have five minutes.

Step 2: Ask each recorder to report to the entire group. The first recorder reads the list of ideas from her or his team. Write the ideas on newsprint as this recorder reports. Remaining recorders read only new ideas (no repeats).

Step 3: As you close, ask each young person to tell which idea he or she will try during the next week. Plan for a follow-up conversation to hear how they did.

Variation: Ask each youth to write on a sticky note a commitment he or she would like to make to display at home as a reminder.

This activity originally appeared in Rebecca Grothe, More Building Assets Together *(Search Institute, 2002).*

4

CARING
NEIGHBORHOOD

Young person experiences caring neighbors.

**Thirty-seven percent of youth in grades 6 through 12
believe that there are people in their neighborhood who
care about them. Sixty-three percent do not.**

This information is based on data collected on 148,189 students surveyed in 2003
using *Search Institute Profiles of Student Life: Attitudes and Behaviors*.

When you think of the neighborhood where you grew up, what do you remember? Was there a neighbor who was always sitting outside when you walked by? Were there neighbors who greeted you by name and knew your whole family? Did you have neighborhood friends you could play with on a summer evening?

Research suggests that vulnerable youth in healthy communities have better outcomes than those in unhealthy communities. For many youth, their neighborhoods are one of the places they find those caring adults who become positive influences in their lives.

If you grew up in a friendly and supportive neighborhood, you may be wondering why your neighborhood today seems so different. Many changes have contributed to the fact that neighborhoods are not the same for our young people as they were for us when we were growing up. Changes in architectural styles have led to the disappearance of front porches or even front steps, where neighbors could keep an eye on what was happening and could chat with friends walking by. People who have automatic garage door openers may rarely or never interact with neighbors outside. The average American adult now works a 46-hour workweek, and 38 percent work more than 50 hours per week. Parents are encouraged to enroll their children in formal after-school programs and sports to build their skills and their résumés, so children spend less time playing unstructured games with neighbors. Add to all of this the anxiety that many parents feel about the possibility of an unknown adult harming their child, and it is no wonder that we all, youth and adults, feel less connected in our own neighborhoods.

And yet, all across North America, individuals and families are taking creative steps to connect with their neighbors and build the relationships that can create a web of support for both young people and adults.

How can you start building the Caring Neighborhood asset for young people?

In My Family

Your children are always watching you. Do you know the neighbors on your block or in your apartment building? If you do, it makes it easier for your children to know them and to see their neighborhood as a caring place. Model what it looks like to be a good neighbor.

If you have elderly neighbors, talk to your children about how you can be helpful to them. Perhaps you can offer to rake leaves for them in the fall or share vegetables from your garden. Invite them over for cookies and tea and get to know them. Ask how long they have lived in the neighborhood. If they have been there for many years, ask them what changes they have witnessed over that time. This can be a great learning experience for your children and is a way for your neighbor to get to know you as well. After the visit ask your children if they can think of any other ways your family could connect with your neighbors.

If a new family moves into your neighborhood or building, ask your children what you could do as a family to help them feel welcome. If you've noticed that the new family has children, think about what they might want to know about the area they have moved to. Depending on the ages of your children, you might take over a plate of cookies, or a complete meal you have prepared together. Give the neighbors tips on child-friendly parks, stores, and restaurants. Encourage your children to go with you to welcome your new neighbors.

Ask your children whether there are places in your neighborhood that they feel safe and anywhere they feel unsafe. Ask them what makes a place feel safe or unsafe. If they do feel uncomfortable in some area and can explain why they feel that way, discuss whether it is something that can be changed. Perhaps an intersection is too busy to safely cross and your family can contact city hall to inquire about the rules governing stoplights and stop signs. Maybe it's an area that is poorly lit at night. Document it and have a conversation with someone in your local government. Encourage your children to participate so they can see how problems can be identified and addressed.

Other ways to participate in your neighborhood include checking with your city to see if it sponsors Neighborhood Watch or Neighborhood Block Club programs. Many cities offer resources and training to groups of residents willing to be involved in their local area. Ask if your children can participate with you.

Some neighborhoods have residents' groups that publish a local newsletter or sponsor local events. Encourage them to include youth as writers and on event planning committees.

Remember that one way children feel they are part of a caring neighborhood is through teaching them how to be caring neighbors.

In My Professional Life

If you work with young people in a school or an out-of-school setting, there are many ways you can support them in building a more caring neighborhood for themselves.

Encourage youth to talk about their neighborhood and identify the adults they could go to if they were locked out of their home, or had another problem that required help from an adult.

Ask youth to make a map of their neighborhood and note something interesting about each neighbor they know.

Have young people identify a neighbor they would like to get to know better. Have them come up with strategies for meeting and getting acquainted with their neighbors.

Have age-appropriate conversations about being safe in their neighborhood. Many police departments have programs they can offer in school or after-school settings. Contact your police department to see if a representative would be willing to meet with your group of students.

Ask young people to write about or talk about a time when they were "good neighbors." What did they do or say? What is something else they could do to be good neighbors to someone in their neighborhood?

Focus on the physical neighborhood. Are there places where young people feel particularly safe? Are there places that feel unsafe? Brainstorm possible solutions if they identify problems.

Make a list of neighborhood service projects students could engage in. Work with them to plan an activity. It could be cleaning up neighborhood trash, planting a garden, sponsoring a block party so neighbors can meet each other, or planning a chore day when teens rake lawns, change storm windows, or paint for elderly neighbors. Some communities run a volunteer chore service and can arrange for equipment or have a list of people in need of assistance.

In My Community

You may have seen the bumper sticker that says, "Start Seeing Motorcycles." Imagine that you have a bumper sticker with the message "Start Seeing Young People." Begin by reflecting on your neighborhood. If you live in a city, this might be the apartment building in which you live. If you live outside the city center, you might think of your neighborhood in terms of the blocks of houses radiating out from yours. In the country, it might be several miles encompassing your nearest neighbors.

Draw a picture of your neighborhood. As you mentally work your way across every home, mark every household you can identify that has children or teenagers in it. Give yourself a point for every young person's name you can attach to one of those households.

How did you do? What can you do to learn more about the young people in your neighborhood? Take a mental walk through your day. Do you know the young person who bags your groceries at the supermarket? Who hands you your clothes at the dry cleaner? Who delivers your newspaper? Who prepares your latte at the coffee shop? Where else do you cross paths with young people in your neighborhood?

While it might seem that building the Caring Neighborhood asset is a big task, it all starts with making simple connections. And connections often begin with simple conversations. Think about the neighbors you'd like to know better. Do you know their names? Do they have any pets? Do you know some of the children's interests? Maybe you have noticed young people getting in the car with hockey bags or basketballs or musical instruments. Perhaps you have observed your neighbors gardening or walking their dog. Any one of these bits of information is enough to ask a question to start a conversation:

- When's your next hockey game? How is your team doing this season?

- Are you in the school orchestra? What composers do you like?

- What's your dog's name? How long have you had it?

- Those flowers are beautiful. Are they hard to grow?

Stranger Anxiety

Because some parents are anxious about their children talking to strangers, it is wise to start by introducing yourself to them before starting a conversation with their child. Tell them a bit about yourself—where you work (if you are working), what hobbies you have, and so on. Tell them about a neighbor who had an impact on you when you were growing up. Or note that it can be hard for young people today to befriend their neighbors, because people have such busy lives. Let them know you are interested in making the neighborhood a place whose residents, from youngest to oldest, feel safe and connected. Offer to host a neighborhood potluck where families can socialize and learn more about each other. Some families will be delighted to connect right away. Others may take awhile to respond. Keep trying.

Laura Meverden, the program director with the YMCA in Appleton, Wisconsin, and her husband use Halloween as a way to make a special connection with their young neighbors. They make personalized packages for the children they know well. The items in their Halloween bags go beyond candy and include crayons, school supplies, bubble bath, and matchbox cars.

"We also encourage our teenage neighbors to come," Laura says. "Our rule is it does not matter how old you are—as long as you're in costume."

Try this yourself—learn the birthdays of some of the young people in your neighborhood and make sure to send them a card or small gift, or leave a May Day basket at their door.

Welcoming New Neighbors

If you have lived in your neighborhood for a while, you have a wonderful opportunity to set the tone when a new family moves in. Think about how you would like to welcome them. Try any of the following friendly gestures:

Introduce yourself by delivering a batch of cookies or a cake. If you live in an apartment building, post a sign or drop off a note to welcome new neighbors.

Deliver a small bouquet of flowers from your garden, if you have one. If you don't, grab an inexpensive bunch from your neighborhood drugstore or gas station.

If you live in a cold environment, help your neighbors shovel snow.

Make a short list of services available nearby, such as the nearest hardware store, car mechanic, babysitters, Laundromat, pizza parlor, library, or whatever you think would help them connect to resources in the area.

If you run into your new neighbors in the hallway of your apartment building, ask how things are going and offer any apartment-specific tips you have; for example, you have to pull the door toward you as you turn the key, or the dryer fries your clothes if you leave them in for longer than 30 minutes. Let them know you're available to answer any questions they may have.

Offer to babysit their children from time to time, or to feed their cats or fish while they're away. If their children are alone for a few hours after school, offer your home as a friendly place for them to hang out until their parents get home.

If there are a number of new families that haven't connected yet, ask them if they would like to help you plan a block party. Most cities have someone on staff that can tell you what the regulations are and what resources they might provide to help you plan your event. This can be a great way to bring everyone together at once so adults and young people can start connecting. You could also ask some of the teens or preteens to help you plan activities that would appeal to them at the block party.

An alternative to a block party for apartment dwellers is to organize a progressive dinner, depending on how many units are in your building. If you live in a multiplex, you might ask just the closest residents on your floor, or if you live in a building with fewer units, try to include all of your neighbors. Keep it simple: Start at one apartment for cheese and crackers, move to another for a dinner of pizza, and end the evening with cookies and coffee at a third apartment. Plan to rotate a few times a year—for example, have apartments 3A, 3B, and 3C host in October, then ask apartments 3D, 3E, and 3F to host in February. If you live in a large complex that has a community room or party room, you might want to gather there first as an icebreaker for neighbors who are reluctant to bring people into their apartments.

If You *Are* the New Neighbor

If you have moved into a new neighborhood and want to be part of the web of caring adults who make young people feel safe and known, look for opportunities to introduce yourself. If you have a yard, spend time outside and chat with people while they're walking their dogs. Ask local teens about the best place to go for pizza, to grab a good cup of coffee, or to see a movie. If you have moved to a house with a basketball hoop, offer its use to the neighbor kids. If you have moved to an apartment, invite neighbor kids to draw pictures to decorate your door.

Your neighbors might appear aloof, but perhaps they are just shy. If they don't make the first move, go ahead and introduce yourself.

STORIES OF SUPPORT

On August 1, 2007, Minneapolis–St. Paul residents—and people from around the world—were stunned to hear that a major Interstate bridge had collapsed into the Mississippi River during the evening rush hour. Only a 15-minute drive away, Nathan Eklund and his wife were about to host a backyard puppet show through Open Eye Figure Theater in Minneapolis.

The puppeteers were already setting up their show in our backyard when the skies turned overcast. We were nervous. We were expecting a large group of neighborhood families, and our house was not going to be sufficient if we had to move the show indoors. I spent most of the afternoon and evening on the Internet and Weather Channel watching cells moving through the area. By some very fine luck, it looked like our show was going to happen directly during a lull in the dark weather.

As families started arriving, I turned on the TV one last time to check the weather. And that's when I saw the images that burned into the collective memories of all of us. The 35W bridge had fallen. I sat transfixed, dumbfounded that this was happening fewer than five miles from our home.

I stepped into our backyard and told the performers and the early arrivers the news. None of us could believe what we were hearing. Then the neighbors started drifting in, vacant-eyed as they too tried to handle the juxtaposition of a backyard full of excited kids watching puppets and a horrifying tragedy happening only miles away.

During the puppet show, the sounds of sirens and helicopters served as the background to the show. Squeals of laughter and the lilting tunes coming from the accordion of the puppet troupe blended somewhere above our heads with the frantic sounds of rescue.

And throughout the surreal experience, I couldn't help but be struck by a profound sense of gratitude that at this most horrible moment, we had a backyard of community members with whom to share the experience. Afterward, people lingered in our backyard for a longer than usual period, as if to delay momentarily returning to far more sobering times.

Considering that the impetus for hosting the show in the first place was to meet members of the community and make connections for our children, the evening was a tremendous success—one that accentuated our collective happiness in having a community and one that cemented our gratitude for the strength of having others on whom to rely. My memory of that night is not of two distinct moments; rather, I have one amalgam of the sadness of loss and thankfulness for the power of community.

Building Deeper Connections with a Young Neighbor

For many young people, the adults in their lives cycle through and are then gone. A teacher is in their life for 9 months. A coach might spend time with them for 8 to 12 weeks. With grandparents and other extended family members often living far away, neighbors are sometimes the only adults, apart from their parents, who are in close contact with a young person over many years.

Think about your own life. Were there times when you were frustrated or felt alone? As you watch the young people growing up in your neighborhood, think about how you could support one specific young person. Does she play a sport? Go to some of her games. Is he in the school band or orchestra? Take in the spring concert. Is she active in theater? Attend a performance. Over time you will be forming a relationship built on shared experiences.

Now think a little deeper. Are there any interests you and your young neighbor share? Maybe he has asked you questions about your garden as you work in your yard. Ask him to help you and teach him about the plants you are growing.

Do you like to work on your car engine, tune up your lawn mower, or fix broken appliances? If a young neighbor shows an interest in your hobbies, let her watch you in action so she can learn what you are doing.

Do you like to read or knit or cook? Whatever your hobby, it might be of interest to a young person living nearby. Share a pattern, a recipe, a book. Name a day and time that you like to pursue your hobby and invite him to join you. If he is younger, ask him to come with a parent at first so everyone can get to know each other. If you're already getting together with a group of neighborhood adults to pursue a shared interest, invite some of your younger neighbors to join in on occasion.

Pace Yourself

Are you feeling a little overwhelmed at the thought of too much connection? There are many ways to start with single events and work your way toward a level of connection you feel comfortable maintaining. And remember, neighbor kids and their families are generally not looking for another weekly meeting to add to their calendars. The sporadic nature of neighborhood relationships can be part of their charm. You see each other frequently for a while, and then diverge. When you next connect, you have new stories to share and things to catch up on. Here are some activities you can try:

Suggest a neighborhood cleanup day in the spring or fall and invite everyone to clean up some common areas—such as the street or neighborhood park—or their own yards and then join you in the afternoon for lemonade and cookies to celebrate.

If you have lots of elementary school–age children in your neighborhood, talk to the parents about holding a parade, and invite the children over in advance to add crepe paper streamers or other decorations to their outfits or bikes. Work with some of the older children to write invitations to neighbors so they can join in the fun as well.

Organize a neighborhood bake sale or garage sale, or try a barter day—you and your neighbors can gather to trade items.

Host an afternoon of games or arts and crafts. Ask another neighbor to help, and make another connection. Depending on the ages of the young people in the neighborhood, it could be as simple as Sidewalk Games Day, or more advanced, depending on your own interests and those of the young people.

Sidewalk Games Day—Supply chalk and let the children draw pictures or hopscotch squares on the sidewalk. Add a jump rope and join if you remember some of the rhymes!

Craft for a Cause Day—Invite teens to join you in knitting scarves for a nearby homeless shelter, making fleece blankets for a community teen shelter, or making baby caps or blankets for an area hospital to distribute. (Simple free patterns for all these projects and suggestions for more can be found on the Internet or at your local library.)

Keep it simple. If you have a lawn, set up your sprinkler on a hot day and invite children to come play in it. If you live in an apartment building, take kids some ice water or lemonade while they are playing outside. On a cold day, offer your yard for sledding or making snowmen, and then host a warm-up session complete with hot chocolate and marshmallows.

One suburban mother of three young girls came up with easy ideas for activities for neighborhood children. She set up a taffy pull on a picnic table in her back yard and let the children make their own candy. They pulled and stretched the taffy until it was ready to cut into pieces, and then she let the children take their candy home. You can find recipes for saltwater taffy and interesting science facts about the ingredients on the Internet at sites such as exploratorium.edu. Another time she had children create rock candy by suspending a clean cotton string in a glass jar filled with a mixture of sugar and water. For the recipe and process, search for "rock candy" at exploratorium.edu.

Talking to Young People—Where Do I Start?

Adults can sometimes be very predictable in conversations with youth. We ask about school. We comment on how the youth have grown. We ask vague questions. Here are some tips that were developed by

Taylor, Elana, Laura, and Erica—four 11-year-olds in St. Louis Park, Minnesota—to help us do better.

Talking with Kids and Teens—A Quick Guide

- Be yourself. Don't pretend to be someone you're not.

- Treat us as equals.

- Ask about things we can both relate to—movies, books, world events.

- Be specific when you ask questions.

- Don't try too hard just to make us like you. We like it when you are yourself.

- Don't start conversations with "You're getting so tall!" "What's new?" or "How's school?"

Relationships Are Reciprocal

As you get to know young people in your neighborhood, you may think you're doing all the work. But if you stop and pay attention, you may be able to identify some of the things you are gaining as well.

When you start building a friendship with someone who is younger than you, you are able to remember and share stories from your own past. You are also able to catch a glimpse into what it means to be a young person today—different from your own experiences in some ways, but very similar in others.

Being in a relationship with a young person keeps us on our toes. They can tell when we are only half paying attention, and as the friendship deepens, they may feel comfortable calling us on that behavior.

Young people will sometimes ask us deep questions about life and death and relationships and all the other issues we wrestle with over our lifetime. They care about our answers because they are building their own. It is sometimes easier to go out on a limb and share our own uncertainties with them, rather than admitting them to a peer. And they challenge us, so we have an opportunity to refine our own answers.

And frankly, it is just plain fun to have friends of all ages.

ACTIVITY 1

Neighborly Advice

Focus: Youth offer suggestions for healthy neighborhood relationships.

Before the group arrives: Write each of these skit starters on a sheet of paper or index card:

- Today after school, you watch your 5-year-old sister and her friend. You take them with you to help rake your neighbor's lawn. After a while, you notice a huge bunch of flowers they are carrying—picked from your neighbor's garden. What do you do now?

- When you got off the bus last Thursday, you noticed people carrying boxes into the apartment two doors down. It's Monday now, and you see two kids you don't know playing in front of your building after school. What do you do now?

- The woman who lives next door is sweeping her front walk. Her husband died last summer. You try to be friendly when you see her, and she always wants you to stop and talk. Some days, you just don't have time to visit with her. Today is one of those days. What do you do now?

Step 1: Form three teams and give each team one of the skit starters. Challenge teams to plan a skit that shows a course of action that would be a positive experience for everyone involved in the situation. Allow about 10 minutes for teams to work, then ask each team to present its skit.

Step 2: Ask the following questions:

- Was it challenging to think of solutions that are positive for everyone involved? Why or why not?

- What gets in the way of positive relationships in your neighborhood?

- What are the three most important things that people of all ages can do to create and maintain a caring neighborhood?

This activity originally appeared in Rebecca Grothe, More Building Assets Together *(Search Institute, 2002).*

ACTIVITY 2

Important Contact

You will need:

- writing paper for each youth
- pen or pencils—one for each youth

Focus: Youth initiate a conversation with an adult neighbor after deciding what to talk about with that person.

Set the stage: Have each youth identify one adult neighbor he or she would like to call or visit within the next few days. Explain that after making contact with that person, each youth will report back to the group on how it went.

Tell participants that the purpose of this contact is to build two-way communication. Ask them to list four or five questions they would like to ask their neighbor. Have them work in pairs so they can help each other create their lists, but also encourage youth to make their lists based on what they know about this neighbor. For example, youth might ask: I know you like woodworking. What projects have you been working on lately? What did you think of how the Knicks played yesterday?

Then have youth find a different partner and identify two things happening in their own lives that they could talk about with this neighbor. For example, youth might list school, work, band, the novel they're reading, and sports.

Tell youth that even if the neighbor doesn't ask questions, they must tell about those two things. Then have youth make their contacts.

After youth report on their experiences, ask:

- What did you do? Describe the experience.
- What did you learn?
- Did the neighbor ask you many questions? How did that make you feel?
- How did the neighbor respond when you told her or him what was happening in your life? How did that response make you feel?
- Were you surprised by anything that happened during your conversation?
- Do you want to have another conversation with this neighbor? Why or why not?
- Who else could you do this activity with?

This activity originally appeared in Jolene L. Roehlkepartain, Building Assets Together *(Search Institute, 1997).*

CHAPTER
5

CARING SCHOOL CLIMATE

School provides a caring and encouraging environment.

Twenty-nine percent of youth in grades 6 through 12
reported that they experience a caring school climate.
Nearly half (47 percent) of youth in grade 6 in the survey
experienced a caring school climate. That percentage drops
to 35 percent by grade 7 and to 25 percent by grade 9,
rising just slightly to 28 percent by grade 12.

This information is based on data collected from 148,189 students surveyed in 2003
using *Search Institute Profiles of Student Life: Attitudes and Behaviors.*

Some adults are quick to dismiss the Caring School Climate asset
as "nice but not necessary" if their school environments put major
emphasis on content mastery and test scores. However, many researchers have studied the impact of the support provided in a school setting
and have linked caring school climate not only to better academic performance but also to better mental health (less anxiety and depres-
sion) and lower delinquency (fewer suspensions from school, better
school attendance, less substance use) in adolescents.[8]

Search Institute's research team has identified three components that make up what young people experience as a caring school climate. First, students need to feel that their teachers care about them. Teachers play a unique role in students' lives. Not only are they charged with conveying new learning to students, but they must also evaluate how successful students have been in mastering that content—even though students vary widely in their degrees of interest in the material, their learning styles, and their preparation for learning. Students who have fallen short on previous evaluations may not be open to new learning or may lack confidence in their ability to learn. This places great responsibility on the teacher to create a classroom climate that encourages students to let go of past shortcomings and look forward to learning new content.

The second component that makes up a caring school climate is the encouragement young people experience in their school. Much of that encouragement comes from their classroom teachers, because they spend so much time with them, but it will also ideally come from other adults who interact with students, including administrators, counselors, school nurses, cafeteria workers, classroom aides, custodians, coaches, bus drivers, and classroom volunteers.

The third component of a caring school climate is a young person's sense that other students in their school care about them. This is one of the reasons that antibullying programs can play such an important part in creating a caring school climate. The bullied student isn't the only one affected—student bystanders may also find themselves doubting that their classmates care about each other.

In My Family

Talking about the importance of a caring school climate with your children is a great way to see their school through their eyes. Ask them what they think a caring school climate is. What does it look like? Sound like? Feel like? When they think about positive experiences at school, do they think of specific people? Who are those people? Are they teachers or other staff? Are they other students?

First, help them identify adults who care about them at school. For one 14-year-old, it was the man who came every week to fill the vending machine. This man always made time for a short conversation and had no expectations of the teen. The boy identified him as someone who made school feel like a caring place.

Talk to your kids about how students care about each other, too. Ask them if most of their classmates get along and support each other. If the answer is no, ask them for ideas about how that might be changed.

For many young people, the chance to talk through what makes their school feel caring or uncaring is a first step in helping them address changes they would like to see. For some, it is an opportunity to get beyond what school "feels" like and to actually identify steps they can take to improve the place they spend so many hours each day.

Celebrate your child's successes at school. Identify and thank the adults who offer your child support at school. If you have time during the day, volunteer at your local school. Be a part of making the school a caring place for students. See Chapter 6 for more ideas.

In My Professional Life

Most students know that school is important. For all of them it consumes a major portion of their day and their thoughts. When something is going poorly for them, they may cope by talking about school as a waste of time, or a teacher as unfair or mean. They might comment that they hate a student who was formerly a friend. It won't help to jump in with a quick contradiction at this point. What they are saying is that they are frustrated or feeling stuck. If you can keep that in mind, you can play a more supportive role by getting past their impassioned first statement and listening to their story. If they can tell their story without interruption, some of the energy often starts to diminish and they are ready to start looking ahead to next steps.

Without amplifying or dismissing their story, you can now begin asking questions that will help them reframe the situation and get some perspective. You will be most helpful when you ask questions that clarify factual information: Did your teacher say you got an F for the semester or on this assignment? Did your teacher suggest you could rewrite that paper and possibly improve your grade, even if you can't still get an A? Is it possible to do an extra credit assignment to offset that test score?

You can also help a young person gain perspective on the scope of the problem. Listen for use of words like "never" and "always" as points where clarification might reduce the magnitude of the issue.

Refer to the following chart for ideas on how to respond to a young person who's trying to deal with some problems.

Instead of . . .	Try . . .
I can't believe you did/said that!	How did [the other person] respond to that?
Don't worry. It will all blow over.	What worries you most about what happened?
Well, of course your teacher was mad.	Why do you think your teacher responded that way?
Your friend didn't really mean that.	Why do you think your friend did/said that?
Everyone gets picked on at school.	Bullying is not OK. Do you have some ideas for how you want to handle this?

If you are working with a group of students and one begins complaining about some problem at their school, odds are that others will nod their heads in agreement. This gives you a great opportunity to engage in a conversation about the characteristics of a caring (or friendly) school and who can influence those characteristics. For example, one group of students may identify an unfriendly school bus, "unfair" teachers, and a lack of support for extracurricular activities other than a few sports teams.

Ask them which issue they can most directly affect, and have them come up with some examples of how they can address the issue. Then ask how they might influence the other two factors, and what other factors are important to building a caring school climate. Have the group brainstorm all the ways they could start to improve the climate in their school. What can they do by themselves? What can they do as a group or in partnership with others? What do they want to try first?

This process not only helps improve school climate but also gives students opportunities to build other assets, such as planning and decision making.

"A Day in the Life," a skit created and presented by a group of junior high school students, demonstrated the power of the many interactions adults and youth have throughout the school day. The students presented two scenarios—a day in which "Molly" didn't feel support from those around her, and a day in which she did. In the first scenario, Molly's mother yells, "Will you *finally* remember to turn in your field trip form?"; the bus driver barks, "Hurry up and sit down so I can get moving"; a staff person in the hallway says, "Stop dawdling and get to class!"; and her teacher announces, "Someone failed to clean up yesterday, so the whole class will be forfeiting free time today."

The actors freeze and all move backward to begin the second scenario. "Good luck on your test today, Molly," says Molly's mom. "Did you find the field trip form I left on the table for you?"; "Hi Molly," says the bus driver. "I think Laura has saved a spot for you"; "Good morning, Molly, you've got just a few minutes to get to class. Nice job on the recycling posters," says the door monitor as Molly enters her school; "Let's talk about the kind of classroom community we want to create," says Molly's teacher. "I think we need to review some of the rules you helped set at the beginning of the year. This classroom works best when we are all working together."

In just five minutes, these students show the difference little moments can make as they add up to a day in the life of a young person.

What's My Role?

When you play a supportive role for young people, without rushing to fix things, you are not only helping them build their own skills and competencies but also affirming that you believe they are capable of acting on their own behalf.

Ask yourself how you're doing when it comes to supporting a caring school atmosphere for all students.

The last time a young person described a troubling situation he faced at school, I:

- Came up with a great solution for him to try.

- Offered to intervene on his behalf.

- Was annoyed and only partially heard him, because he is always complaining about some situation at school when I am trying to get something else done.

- Told him the situation was his own fault.

- Stifled the urge to respond with any of the above, and tried to really listen to what he was trying to say.

Because we have all had our own experiences with school, it is easy for a young person's dilemmas to trigger a quick response from us. Sometimes our urge is to swoop in and rescue him. "How unfair," we think, as his story reminds us of a similar situation we had to deal with. Sometimes his situation is one he has shared with us before, and we are impatient for him to resolve it and move on. Often we know just the strategy that will turn things around. And yet, as asset-building adults, we need to step out of the way and really listen to what the young person has to say.

We all know that, even as adults, when we are in the midst of a frustrating or anxiety-producing situation with a friend or in a work setting, we are not always quick to find a solution or to act on it once we have identified it. As a baby or toddler, when something frustrated us, it was grounds for a good scream. We didn't have the words to describe what was bothering us, and we didn't have the ability to look ahead and weigh various options.

As we started school we had to navigate a whole new set of relationships with both adults and peers. If we were in a self-contained classroom through the elementary grades, we had one teacher and a small number of students to get to know and learn to work with. When we started junior high or middle school, we suddenly had many more teachers, classrooms, and students to deal with and sometimes found ourselves at odds with old friends and struggling to make new friends. All of those memories, both good and bad, can be triggered when a young friend begins to tell us his story.

While growing up and learning to navigate these new situations is normal, that doesn't make it easy. One of the roles you can play is that of neutral listener. Try not to amplify whatever is distressing him. Resist the urge to step in and intercede on his behalf (except on rare occasions when physical or emotional danger is possible). When you are able to play this role well, a young person has a safe space in which to try to understand the situation that occurred and the feelings it generated. Your being a neutral listener also gives the young person space in which to test steps toward a solution.

In My Community

While people working in a school setting are most directly in a position to build this asset, all adults working with young people can contribute to its development. Anytime you are in a conversation with a teen and the topic turns to school, you have the opportunity to listen for signs of a caring school climate and signs of a negative school climate.

If you mentor or tutor young people or work with them in an out-of-school program, you may be the first—and perhaps only—adult they turn to when something is troubling them at school. You can provide young people with the supportive space they need by asking questions and listening while they describe the situation. With your support they may be able to identify solutions.

Sometimes young people can see a solution but are anxious or unsure about how to carry it forward. You can help them break it down into manageable steps, either by discussing various options or role-playing a conversation with them. For instance, you could play the role of teacher if the student thinks talking to a teacher is a good step toward resolving the concern.

Take the First Step

When the residents of Summerland, British Columbia, Canada, learned that there was a gulf between senior citizens and the students in their community, they knew they had to take action.

Seniors were asked if they'd be willing to greet students one to two mornings a week. Many said yes, despite the negative impressions of youth they had gotten from the media. Their perception of students was that they were vandals, criminals, disrespectful, and unmotivated, said Don MacIntyre, the principal of a middle school in Penticton, a neighboring community. The seniors were simply too far removed from the young people in their community—they no longer had children at home and didn't spend much time with young people in general.

"We needed to change the image of kids," MacIntyre said. Part of the problem was that kids had already felt the negative effects of this misperception and didn't feel motivated to close the senior-student gap.

"They said, 'Why should we? They don't like us anyway,'" MacIntrye recalled.

At the beginning of the project, student leaders partnered with the senior volunteers, but eventually the seniors took ownership of the project, and all students in the school became involved. The volunteers personalized their respective school entrances by decorating the area and providing treats for the students. It wasn't long before barriers began to break down. MacIntyre said that about 90 percent of students chose an entryway depending on who the greeter was that day.

The project, MacIntyre said, "spurred a lot more opportunities to close gaps between seniors and students in the community." And, of course, the school climate became friendlier and more positive.

Take Action

There are many ways you can support your local school system. Make a point of taking any of the following steps toward a caring school climate:

- Be vocal in your support of your local schools.

- Contribute to fund-raisers.

- Find out if there are any free performances or games to attend.

- Tune in to local government so that you know which issues are facing the schools in your neighborhood.

- Participate in local elections, and research education-related issues before casting your vote.

ACTIVITY 1

Take Action!

You will need:

- white board or a large piece of butcher paper

Focus: Students feel empowered to take active roles in their schools.

Before the group arrives: Write the following statements on white board or a large piece of paper and hang it on a wall:

- My teacher cares about me.
- I get lots of encouragement at my school.
- Students at my school care about me.
- I know whom I can talk to at school when I have a problem.

Give young people a few minutes to think about the statements, and then ask them how they feel about each one. Once the discussion starts to wind down, ask these discussion questions:

- Which one would you like to see improved? What could you do to improve it?
- Which one would take other people's help to improve?
- Name some adults or other students at your school who you think might be interested in helping improve school climate.
- How might you ask them for their help? What actions would you suggest?
- How will you know that change is occurring? What will a "caring school climate" look like?

Hall Talk

You will need:

- index cards in three colors
- pencils or pens
- white index cards

Focus: Youth consider how what they say affects school climate.

Before the group arrives: Write each of these situations on a white index card.

- I see a basketball player who hurt her knee in the last game. She's walking with a cane. I say . . .
- I meet a friend who has a new haircut that is way too short. I say . . .
- I bump into a kid I don't recognize and he drops his books. I say . . .
- My locker is jammed and I am late for English. I say . . .
- A friend gave a wrong answer to a question on the oral quiz in math class and feels bad about it. I say . . .
- A classmate says something that I know is an insult against me. After class I say . . .
- I see someone I don't know really well being pushed around by a bully. I say . . .
- I'm running an errand for the coach, and a teacher asks me why I'm not in class. I say . . .
- A boy or girl asks me to a dance, but I really don't want to go with him/her. I say . . .
- I need to use the office phone to call my mom, but the new secretary says, "Use the pay phone." I say . . .

Set the stage: Give each youth one blank colored index card, making sure that the three colors are distributed evenly among your group. Tell youth that they will take turns drawing a situation card, reading it aloud, and then calling out one of the three colors of cards. Youth who have a card in the color named stand and give a possible response to the situation.

Step 1: After each situation and possible responses, ask the rest of the group to choose the responses they feel would be most likely to improve school climate in the hallways and classrooms.

Step 2: Ask youth the following questions:

- How do the things people say to each other affect school climate?
- What can be done to encourage youth and adults in school to be more positive when they talk to each other and about each other?

This activity originally appeared in Rebecca Grothe, More Building Assets Together *(Search Institute, 2002).*

CHAPTER
6

PARENT INVOLVEMENT
IN SCHOOLING

*Parent(s) are actively involved in helping
young person succeed in school.*

**Twenty-nine percent of youth in grades 6 through 12
say that their parent(s) ask about and help them with
schoolwork, talk to them about what they are doing in
school, and go to meetings or events at school.**

This information is based on data collected from 148,189 students surveyed in 2003
using *Search Institute Profiles of Student Life: Attitudes and Behaviors*.

An important factor in improving student academic performance is
the support young people receive at home from the adults who are
raising them. Studies have shown that when parents are firm yet
warm, and communicate effectively, their children develop a sense of
self-worth and believe they can do well in school, which leads to better grades. Other studies have shown that parent involvement in their
child's education is twice as powerful as family income in predicting
the child's academic success.

Parent involvement at the middle school and secondary levels is
usually lower than involvement levels during the elementary grades.

The curriculum becomes more complicated. Schools are larger, and there are more teachers to keep track of. Students are looking for more independence. Parents who stayed at home in their children's early years are more likely to be employed as their children grow older. All these reasons add to the challenges schools face with regard to engaging parents in children's education in the middle and upper grades. Yet, the research is clear. Having parents who stay involved makes a big difference for young people.

In a research brief written by the Harvard Family Research Project[9] (2007), three processes are identified as making a difference in student outcomes:

Parenting. "Warm, responsive parenting in adolescence is related to school success and positive social and emotional outcomes." Adolescents show higher self-reliance, school performance (GPA), and career aspirations when their parents are supportive. In a study of low-income students, the degree to which mothers encouraged their 11-year-olds to make independent decisions predicted the high school graduation rates of those students.[10]

Another aspect of parenting involves monitoring. When parents keep track of their child's comings and goings, their child is less likely to have school problems and more likely to earn good grades.

Home-School Relationships. Teacher-parent and school-parent communication plays a role by keeping parents in touch with academic requirements and how their child is doing. Attendance at school functions has a positive impact on adolescent academic achievement. Both of these strategies communicate the importance parents place on education.

Responsibility for Learning Outcomes. Research shows that when parents continue to encourage completion of homework throughout adolescence, their child's grades are better. When parents have high academic expectations, their children complete a higher number of high school credits, and encouraging college attendance is associated with a higher probability that students will take college-preparatory courses in high school and then enroll in college.

In My Family

Ask yourself the following questions about your child's education.

Question: *Where does your child complete her or his homework?*

Make sure your child's homework space is free of major distractions (for example, in a quiet area rather than facing the television).

Equip the homework space with the basics so a lack of equipment doesn't prevent your child from doing homework. Supplies vary depending on the age of the child. You may have received a supply list at the beginning of the school year that suggested specific items. Generally, all students will need paper, pencils or pens, scissors, a ruler, calculator, markers, and a dictionary. If your child is at an age where she is being assigned major papers or projects that need to be worked on in stages, give her a calendar to keep track of deadlines. If your child needs to use a computer to do homework, place it in a public area of the house rather than in your child's bedroom so you can monitor the sites she visits and help her stay on task. If you do not have a computer at home, establish a regular time for your child to visit the local library to use computers for homework assignments. Also check with the school to see if it provides access to computers before or after school.

Try to establish a routine time for homework. If homework is to be done before any evening television shows are turned on, for example, that rule will lessen arguments about turning off the television and pleas for "just one more show." It also lets your child know that you place a high value on education and that homework comes first.

Know your child. If he or she needs some downtime or a snack before being able to concentrate on homework, allow time for that, but do establish a regular routine.

Question: *How well do you stay informed about your child's homework?*

Try to meet your child's teachers early in the year. Find out what their expectations are for homework completion.

Read school newsletters sent home early in the school year to see if there is a Web site or phone number to call for homework assignments. This is less likely as your son or daughter moves into the high school years, but check to be sure.

Place copies of any calendars or syllabi your child receives in a folder where you can both refer to it on evenings when your child says there is "no homework."

Ask your child what homework she has, and help her plan ahead for major assignments. Planning and decision making are key skills young people learn during their teens. If your child has a major paper due in four weeks, for example, ask her what days she wants to schedule to do any necessary research and outlining, what deadline she wants to set for a rough draft, and what days she wants to use for editing and revising. These are not natural skills for any of us, and we learn them by using them over and over until they become habits.

If you struggled in school and still find it difficult to support your child's after-school learning, enroll her in a tutoring program or seek out a mentor who is willing to play this role. Many children are more responsive to academic assistance from an adult other than their parents.

Question: *How do you keep track of deadlines for forms that must be returned, test dates your child should be prepared for, field trip days, and the dates for any extracurricular activities your child is engaged in?*

Consider how you would like to organize this information. Some school districts send out a calendar to all families with major events already marked. If not, you should decide if you want to keep a separate calendar for all school-related dates, or whether you wish to include them in your personal calendar.

Some families keep a folder or three-ring binder to organize all the various forms and flyers sent home by school, or post them on a bulletin board. Others designate a shelf or drawer for school information or use a heavy magnetized clip on the refrigerator. Think about what system will work best for you.

Question: *How do you let your child know that her or his education is important to you?*

Consistently reinforce a regularly scheduled homework time.

While you are preparing or eating dinner, ask your child to teach you something interesting he learned that day.

Invite your child to share dreams and hopes about his future. Encourage him to find out what kinds of classes will support him in reaching that dream. Know that your child's goals will change over the years, but the act of imagining himself as a successful adult in the future is a good way to help him see the value of education.

Encourage family reading time. Reading for pleasure has been squeezed out of many teens' lives by all the other competing demands, but it is a strong predictor of academic success. Some families establish a reading hour one or two days a week. Others share interesting articles they have read with each other. You can encourage your child's reading habits by modeling your own pleasure reading. Remember, reading for pleasure can include magazines, technical manuals, comic books, and nonfiction. Literacy experts say a variety of reading materials can help improve reading skills.

Model an interest in lifelong learning by tackling a new skill or gaining information through a correspondence course, community or evening class, or self-directed study. Share what you've learned with your child.

When your child expresses interest in a career, whether it is to be an engineer, a dancer, or a rock star, ask her what skills she thinks she will need to pursue that particular job and how she might build those skills. You can also help stretch her thinking by pointing out that the engineer needs to be able to write up findings and present them, the dancer may have to understand something about marketing and publicity, and the rock star may need to know how to manage money and understand geography. Tying academic subjects to real-world goals can make the skills learned in school seem more relevant.

In My Professional Life

If you work in a school setting and want to encourage parents' engagement in their children's education, try the following strategies.

Share information about how parental engagement is shown to have a positive effect on learning. In addition to the research mentioned at the beginning of this chapter, several organizations have created specific information you can share with parents about how to be engaged in their child's schooling. The National Education Association (NEA) has suggestions for parents at every grade level: www.nea.org/parents/ppower.html.

The NEA has also developed a series of tip sheets and resources for parents to help them find ways to become more engaged: www.nea.org/parents/resources-parents.html.

Give parents ideas for keeping track of their children's homework assignments. Some schools post assignments on the school's Web site. Teachers may leave a message on their phone each night or week listing the major projects students should be working on. Most students are expected to record their assignments in planners given out at school or purchased by parents. Remind parents that teachers increasingly are using e-mail newsletters and their own Web sites to list both homework and grades.

Remind parents that even though their children may be growing more independent, parents still need to support their children's education by monitoring homework completion, having more conversations about post–high school plans (for college and/or work), and working on planning and decision-making skills.

Encourage parents to attend parent-teacher conferences. Send a reminder the week before the appointment and let them know you are available to answer any questions they may have. Parents should work with their children's teachers toward school success for their child.

Volunteering for the School

Another way parents can be involved in their children's education is to provide much-needed help at school. Even in middle schools and high schools, the tasks always outnumber the hours in a teacher's day. Parents are a genuine source of support even if they are not physically present in the classroom as they may have been during their children's elementary years.

Talk with other staff in your building. Identify types of support you need and include them on a volunteer form or send home a special request. Parents are busy people, so they may be more interested in a one-time project than consistent volunteer hours throughout the year. Try to have a mix of options for participation—some during school hours, some that can be done at home, some that are ongoing, and some that are one-time only. Be specific about time commitments to avoid misunderstandings.

Make sure you thank parents for their help throughout the year. Ask students to help you by writing notes on homemade cards. Acknowledging parents' volunteer efforts not only will help with recruitment and retention of volunteers, but it is also a way to let students see that you value their parents' participation in their education.

Things That Get in the Way

Parents fall away from supporting their children's education for all sorts of reasons. Some of them are things you have no control over, such as a family crisis or juggling multiple jobs. But there are some factors over which you *can* have an influence:

I don't know what their homework assignment is.

How will you notify parents of major homework assignments (syllabus at the beginning of a class, posting on the school Web site, posting on your voice mail, sending e-mail)?

How can parents contact you if they have questions or concerns about homework, and how will you make them feel welcome to do so?

I don't understand their homework and can't answer their questions.

Make "crib sheets" for parents, such as a handout with some basic math formulas on it, helpful Web sites, or overview questions they can ask their children as they are working on a particular assignment.

Host a "Homework Help for Parents Night," an evening when parents can learn about the subject you teach or ask questions about how they can provide homework support.

Give parents tips so they can support the process you want students to use when doing their homework. Share some specific questions or statements parents can use to get their child started on homework, even if they don't know the content of the assignment.

Post information and suggestions related to current areas of study on your school's Web site and encourage parents to consult the resource regularly. You can post a "Help!" link to your e-mail address so parents can submit specific questions.

I'm helping my child with homework, but we are having a hard time getting motivated.

Periodically include homework assignments that young people can do with their families, such as an interview in which they remember a current event or a series of questions that students and parents can ask each other. Maybe they can create an art collage or write a poem together. Be creative.

I turned in my volunteer form, but no one ever called me.

If you ask for volunteers, be sure to follow up, even if just to thank parents for volunteering and to tell them you will be contacting them later in the year.

Parents who begin to volunteer early in the school year are easier to hang on to than parents who don't become engaged until much later. If you can't call parents back, add "Willing to be a classroom volunteer coordinator" to the volunteer form and work with a parent who can do the callbacks and scheduling for you. There are parents who love the opportunity to get to know the parents of their child's classmates in this way.

Find ways to appreciate parents for the support they give. Let students participate in this process. Students can:

- Write thank-you notes. It's good practice for life and for writing skills.

- Create volunteer Certificates of Appreciation.

- Plan a small thank-you party at the end of a term or year or after a special event involving multiple volunteers.

Nonschool Settings

If you work with parents and guardians in other settings (congregations, parent education classes, after-school programs), you can still encourage them to be engaged in their children's education. Modify any of the earlier suggestions to fit your setting. If you are teaching a skill or working with a curriculum, many of the same strategies will apply. If you work with parents, but not directly with their children, consider some of the following additional ideas:

- Offer a coffee hour when parents can share how they have been engaged in their children's education.

- Ask parents if they need any help navigating the school system, and find resources for them, where appropriate.

- Affirm them in all they do to support their children's education.

In My Community

There are a variety of ways community members can support parent involvement in schooling.

Neighbors Supporting Families for School Success

If families in your neighborhood have children in school, there are several ways you can support parent involvement in their schooling:

Volunteer to watch younger children on conference days, so parents can focus on what is being said during the teacher conferences.

Ask about school events neighbor children are participating in (music or sports groups, special events) and make an effort to attend once in a while. Offer to help with transportation if that is an issue.

Let parents know that you believe their involvement matters— when their children are young as well as when their children are older. Mention the correlation of parents' involvement to children's academic success.

Ask them how you can support their efforts to stay connected to their child's schools.

If you attended college, offer to talk to the parents or children about your experiences and why you think it is important to go to college.

Businesses Supporting Parent Involvement

Businesses have the unique potential to make a wide-ranging impact on the community, including parent involvement in schooling. Consider which of the following strategies would work well for your organization.

Offer to sponsor or support college information nights for high school students and their parents. Talk to your local high school guidance office to explore how you might do this.

Recognize employees who are engaged parents. Mention how engaged parents increase student academic success, and how student success leads to a prepared workforce.

Offer parents time off to attend parent-teacher conferences or student performances. Or create flex-time options that allow parents to attend and make up work time on another day.

Sponsor bag lunch seminars for employees and invite local school personnel to talk about the impact parent engagement makes on student success.

Think about opportunities that align with your business. For example, printing companies can offer to print bumper stickers for local schools that help parents celebrate their children, such as "My child is an honor roll student at XXX school." If you are in the restaurant business, consider offering specials on the nights of conferences or school events. Invite families to dine in your establishment at a reduced rate. This promotes your business as well as celebrates involved parents.

If your organization is located next to a school and has a parking lot, partner with the school to announce and **offer free parking to parents attending evening or weekend events.**

Faith Communities Supporting Involved Parents

Faith communities already know how important it is to engage parents in their child's education, whether spiritual or academic. Your community can support family engagement in schooling.

- Mention local school events and encourage parents and others to attend.

- Offer babysitting for younger children on school conference nights.

- Celebrate parents for all the positive steps they take to support their child's education.

- Host parent education events that focus on the important role parents play in staying connected with their child's school.

Reaching Out to Immigrant Families

Parents who have recently immigrated to the United States face many challenges when it comes to understanding and becoming involved in their children's education. The California-based Parent Institute for Quality Education (PIQE) recommends using the following guidelines for helping recent immigrants assimilate into the new educational culture in which their children participate.[11]

Accommodate parents' needs. Provide child care, refreshments and snacks, and classes in different languages.

Personally invite parents to attend parent-teacher conferences. Remember details about each family and follow up with specific questions, learn parents' names, and introduce yourself by offering some personal information so parents can contact you outside of school.

Stress the importance of parent involvement. Since parent involvement in schooling is not emphasized in all countries, new strategies must be used to convey the importance of involvement to immigrant parents. When PIQE instructors work with parents, they refer to their children's education as an urgent issue that needs the parents' immediate attention.

Join parents in setting an educational goal for their children. Tell them you are going to work together to ensure their children's advancement to college, and assure them that the goal *is* attainable if they start preparing now.

Many immigrants are too nervous to get involved in their children's education because they are unfamiliar with the school system. Ease these worries by explaining in clear terms the different elements of the educational system: grading and testing, school policies, school and district resources, and parent involvement opportunities. Help parents come up with questions they can ask their children's teachers about how to support their children's learning.

Give parents tips on how they can help their children. For example, recommend that they meet with their children's teachers; show an interest in their children's education by asking questions and offering praise when their children do well; ask their children's teachers how their children have been performing on standardized tests and other projects; and learn about extracurricular programs their children can join.

To get *all* parents more involved, try creating a "Volunteer Talent Form" for them to fill out. See the sample below for ideas.

Sample Volunteer Talent Form

Students whose parents or guardians volunteer at school are more likely to be successful in school and feel more connected to their school. Parents or guardians have many talents that can enhance the learning that goes on at school. Look over the following list and check any talents that you would be interested in sharing:

At school during the day:

☐ I would be willing to meet with a student other than my own child to work on reading or language skills for one hour every week (preferred day and time _____).

☐ I would be willing to meet with a student other than my own child to work on math skills one hour every week (preferred day and time _____).

☐ I am from another country and would be willing to come into a class and share something about my culture, language, or food.

☐ I have spent time in another country and would be willing to come into a class and share something about that country's culture, language, or food.

☐ I have time during the day, so I can come into the school office to help with photocopying, collating materials, or other office projects.

☐ I enjoy writing and would be willing to write or help a small group of students write and assemble a class newsletter.

☐ I enjoy photography or videography and would be willing to come to school to document (or help students document) special events.

☐ I enjoy computer technology and would be willing to provide technical support or develop content for the school Web site.

☐ I would be willing to chaperone a field trip.

Outside School Hours:

☐ I enjoy party planning and would be willing to help organize a potluck dinner for the families in my child's class.

☐ I can sew and would be willing to help with costumes for school plays or other events.

☐ I am interested in helping with a school fund-raiser.

☐ I have talents that haven't been mentioned above and I would be willing to share them. They are _____

_____

My name: _____

My child's name and classroom: _____

Phone number: _____

Best time to reach me: _____ p.m. _____ a.m.

E-mail address: _____

ACTIVITY 1

Parent/Guardian Involvement Reminders

You will need:

- index cards
- markers
- newsprint
- self-stick magnetic tape

Focus: Youth discuss ways to increase parent/guardian involvement in their education.

Set the stage: Ask youth: "What things do your parents/guardians do that let you know they care about your education? What things do parents/guardians do that are not helpful in supporting your education?"

Continue the discussion by asking: "What are other things that parents/guardians could do that would help a young person's education?" As you discuss, make a list of things that parents/guardians can do to be involved in their education in positive ways. For example, talking about what happened in school each day, helping with homework, going to parent-teacher conferences, voting in school-related elections, volunteering for the school, asking how they can help if you aren't getting the grades you want, and sending notes of encouragement to teachers.

Step 1: Invite youth to choose one idea or activity to suggest to their parents/guardians. Pass out index cards and markers for youth to use to make a miniposter with their reminders. Show them how to attach a strip of magnetic tape to the back and encourage them to put the miniposters on their refrigerators at home.

Step 2: Discuss the following questions:

- How will your parents/guardians or other adults at home react to this reminder? What can you do to have a positive discussion about this?
- What are the advantages of having a parent/guardian who is actively helping you succeed in school? What are the drawbacks?
- What advice would you give to parents/guardians who are new to your school?
- What advice would you give to a friend whose parents/guardians are not supportive of her or his activities?

This activity originally appeared in Rebecca Grothe, More Building Assets Together *(Search Institute, 2002).*

ACTIVITY 2

Talk Show Debate

Focus: Youth debate the pros and cons of parent involvement in school.

Set the stage: Ask one youth to be a talk show host, and ask three other youth to serve as guests on the talk show. The rest of the group can be the audience. Explain that the topic of the show is the controversy about parents being involved in their children's school. Assign each of the youth one of these roles:

- One strongly favors parent involvement in school. This person is on the school board, and he or she has been able to introduce some major changes.

- One strongly opposes any parental involvement. This person works two jobs and says he or she pays a lot of taxes for schools to do their jobs.

- One isn't sure but likes to ask a lot of questions and makes points for both sides.

Start the talk show. Encourage the host to "dig for dirt" from the three youth who are serving as guests and to encourage the audience to ask questions and express their opinions. If youth can't think of ways to support their positions, throw out a few ideas to get them going again. After the talk show, ask the group:

- Why do you think only 29 percent of youth nationally have parents who are involved in their schooling?

- In what ways have your own parents been involved in your education (both now and in the past)?

- Would you like for more parents to be involved in your school? Why or why not?

- What are the biggest benefits of parent involvement? Biggest drawbacks? What can you do to encourage parents to be more involved?

This activity originally appeared in Jolene L. Roehlkepartain, Building Assets Together *(Search Institute, 1997).*

Conclusion

Too few young people experience the six assets that make up the Support category. These basic expressions of support across home, school, and neighborhood are crucial building blocks for young people on the path toward healthy adulthood.

Every day young people look at you and other adults, and they wonder, "Do you see me?" "Do I matter to you?" "Will you meet me halfway?" And every day you have a new opportunity to answer these questions with a resounding "Yes!"

As you close this book, think about the next steps you will take to build supportive relationships with young people. And remember that a decade from now, they may be in some gathering where they are asked, "Who made a difference in your life?"

Will you be the person they remember? I believe you will.

Notes

1. P. Hersch, *A Tribe Apart: A Journey into the Heart of American Adolescence* (New York: Ballantine Books, 1999), p. 363.

2. L. Steinberg, J. D. Elmen, and N. S. Mounts, "Authoritative Parenting, Psychosocial Maturity and Academic Success among Adolescents," *Child Development* 60 (1989): 1424–1436.

3. G. W. Peterson and G. K. Leigh, "The Family and Social Competence in Adolescence." In T. P. Gullotta, G. R. Adams, and R. Montemayor (eds.), *Advances in Adolescent Development: Vol. 3. Developing Social Competency in Adolescence,* 97–138 (Newbury Park, CA: Sage, 1990).

4. "My Baby or My Job: Why Elizabeth Vargas Stepped Down," www2.oprah. com/tows/pastshows/200701/tows_past_20070123.jhtml.

5. P. C. Scales and N. Leffert, *Developmental Assets: A Synthesis of the Scientific Research on Adolescent Development,* 2nd ed. (Minneapolis: Search Institute, 2004).

6. Peterson and Leigh, "The Family and Social Competence in Adolescence."

7. FBI, National Center for Missing and Exploited Children, cited in "Teaching Skills, Instilling Confidence Best Ways to Prevent Child Abduction: 'Stranger Danger' Lessons Alone Don't Protect Children," October 4, 2004 (www.mayoclinic. org/news2004-rst/2452.html).

8. Scales and Leffert, *Developmental Assets: A Synthesis of the Scientific Research on Adolescent Development,* 2nd ed., 36–37.

9. H. Kreider, M. Caspe, S. Kennedy, and H. Weiss, "Family Involvement in Middle and High School Students' Education" (Cambridge, MA: Harvard Family Research Project, 2007).

10. H. R. Tenenbaum, et al., "Maternal and Child Predictors of Low-Income Children's Educational Attainment," *Journal of Applied Developmental Psychology,* 28 (2007): 227–238.

11. S. Golan and D. Petersen, "Promoting Involvement of Recent Immigrant Families in Their Children's Education" (Cambridge, MA: Harvard Family Research Project, 2002).

Index

About the Author

Nancy Tellett-Royce is a senior consultant at Search Institute, where she has worked for nearly 10 years. She has provided assistance to many of the nearly 600 communities around the United States and Canada that are a part of Search Institute's Healthy Communities • Healthy Youth (HC • HY) national initiative. She has co-chaired and is currently on the executive committee of Children First in St. Louis Park, Minnesota, which was founded in 1992 as the first HC • HY initiative. Nancy and her husband have two sons, and she is a friend and special adult in the lives of many teenagers. She frequently speaks to groups of parents about the power of Developmental Assets.